D0848408

NATURE IN ENGLISH LITERATURE

NATURE

IN

ENGLISH LITERATURE

EDMUND BLUNDEN

Some have a custom when they bring
  The last of harvest home,
To make the fields with echoes ring
  And joyful to become.
Which was at first, though changed we have
  This joy to brutish mirth,
A triumph to his praise that gave
  The blessings of the earth.

              GEORGE WITHER.

KENNIKAT PRESS
Port Washington, N. Y./London

NATURE IN ENGLISH LITERATURE

First published in 1929
Reissued in 1970 by Kennikat Press
Library of Congress Catalog Card No: 74-113330
ISBN 0-8046-0941-1

Manufactured by Taylor Publishing Company   Dallas, Texas

NOTE

To discover and enunciate the truth of man's inspiration in Nature, as we see it in English poetry and prose, would demand a glorious moment of vision. I have not had one. To give a linked, sustained, and exact chronicle of our writers on Nature would necessitate a library of many thousand volumes, including the *Philosophical Transactions*, *The Field*, and similar works, and a leisure of many thousand hours. I have not had these. Apart from these principal disadvantages, I must take full blame for the defects of the following partial footnotes to a voluminous literature, which I hope to see some vigorous mind investigate in my lifetime. My wish has been to encourage those who have an inclination to read, and be pleased with, some of the many books which have been written in England to the glory of Nature in various views, homely or imaginative; to call attention to merit here and there which, according to my feeling, has not been rewarded with appreciation; and to throw what fresh light I can on some well-known triumphs on the theme of Nature. The omission of studies of masters like Chaucer, Walton, Marvell, Browning, Hardy is deliberate; I hope at a later date to bring together some notes on their work as it affects my present subject.   E. B.

CONTENTS

NATURE IN ENGLISH LITERATURE

I

THE SUBJECT AT LARGE

THE perfection of the shire horse and the mastiff, of the beanfield, the flower-garden, and the great estate, of the avenue of limes and the beeches that crown the hill, of the village green and the heath that refreshes the immense town, are types of that companionship with Nature which the English have commonly enjoyed. The fear of being detected in sentimental mood, which so variously controls the manners of this nation, induces most Englishmen to be averse from considering those excellences and their pleasures as related to the poetry of Wordsworth and Shelley. Their anxiety for their gardens and their boats is not usually summed up by themselves as natural piety. They keep their societies for preserving beautiful places or for preventing the ill-treatment of animals in a different compartment of allusion from "The Ancient Mariner" and "The Beauties of Shakespeare." And yet it is from one luxuriant root that the branches, and leaves, and flowers and fruit of English love of Nature all have their being; the same deep character expresses itself in an abundant variety of occupations, recreations, generosities, and works of science, literature, and art. In its simplest form, it is the boy with his pigeons; and in its finest and fullest realisation it is Crome sharing the evening irradiation of the Poringland Oak, and Wordsworth on the banks of the Wye, listening for the secret of life's "inland murmur." We see that times change, machines multiply, cities outrun the dreams of a century ago, agriculture declines; we lament the collapse of old and venerable parks into mere encampments of gracelessness, and the usurpation of old solitudes by despicable modern kraals, and hurtling land-liners sweeping all before them in lanes where the partridge was safe with her brood all the sunny day. Old liberties are closed by new riches, peace broken by new noises, rusticity depraved into new urbanism. One goes to Bury St Edmunds, and discovers Hodge and Madge at Woolworth's. But the catalogue of "passing away" does not yet hinder this country from being, all points weighed, astonishingly beautiful, mellow with the pleasantest associations, the republic of birds and flowers, the earthly paradise of horse, sheep, heifer, and mongrel, the friendliest meeting-ground of Nature and man; and that this continuous astonishment for the affections and the senses is flourishing in 1929 is in part the highest tribute that the Englishman with all his achievements has ever won. Whether we approach him through his summer holiday or his inheritance of literature, we find him Nature's man.

The inheritance of writings in which English aptitude for every contact with Nature has been made sure is so vast that the Englishman very rarely obtains a view of it, or permits himself to be proud of it. He is like a village oracle, who would just as readily quote for the glory of the parish some gaudy dance-hall rigged up by a speculator as the church with its legended carvings and the barn with its majestic ship-timbers and spacious lights and shadows. He is not always like that, or there would be no call for the present considerations; but "things grown common lose their dear delight." Books which Birket Foster's pure and kind genius has made like the best holiday in Hampshire one ever had were numerous; accordingly they were thrown aside like yesterday's newspapers. But there is more to say on that neglect. The quarter from which enlightenment might have been expected, the department of literary history and criticism, has been much to blame. Involved on every side with tasks similar to those of Mr H. E. Huntington's librarians, our expert bookmen have avoided the larger range of our writers on Nature and country life, perhaps finding it useful to have that immortal question "Is it literature?" always before them. The application of this obscure test to much of our most vivid and healthy rural writing may be compared to the legend that one hears repeated concerning the exclusion of aliens from Australia, where the Chinese coolie desirous of settling is fabled to be given as a language test the composition of an essay in Hebrew. A man writing of the poultry-yard or of threshing or the rules of the weather must be judged according to his humanity, experience, sense of proportion, power of phrase, what you will—but not by the immediate reference to great dramatists, novelists, philosophic stylists. It is the quality of the English race, its contentment, its thoroughness, its way with Nature, that is the importance of so many of the books in my mind. Just as the land is (with all its faults) a masterpiece of bright gardens and spell-binding halls and cottages, that come into view in their scarcely

credible and unboastful felicity of growth, fair as
fancy from chimney-top to lavender-bush, so the
library leading to Walton and White and Wordsworth is able to reward the quiet mind with its
embowered or its upland, georgic or pastoral
excellences.

Chance introduced me, many years since, to a
thick volume lettered *Ellis on Sheep*, which from its
appearance had spent a night or two among the
locust-beans in the troughs of some Sussex flock. I
have since read several disparaging remarks on
William Ellis, farmer of Little Gaddesden, but they
have not overcast the fact that to me Ellis on Sheep
is better than Ruskin on Sheepfolds. The ordinary
prose of the eighteenth century is solid in its words,
that certainly seem rather things than words, but
Ellis is remarkable even in that time for the intensity
of his epithets and the vigour of his verbs. When
his dogs howl in the moonlight, they do so with all
their muscles; when he takes up a handful of soil,
his speech answers the weight, colour, and touch of it.
His anecdotes, his receipts, his cautions are warm
with the passion to make a grazier of the reader; his
hills and vales appear so characteristic that one's
imagination is soon intent on being out there in all
weathers. In short, many of those true stubborn

country expressions which one is delighted to find here and there in Dryden's translation of Virgil's *Georgics* stand out in every chapter of this Ellis; his book is as near to Nature in one aspect as an ostler to the horse he is harnessing. Nothing but breed and use can attain that kind of unity.

Leaving William Ellis to serve as a representative of the sturdy eighteenth-century writers on husbandry (and they are many), I turn to another type of author who has quitted himself well in the service both of Nature and man by knowing and recording animal biography. The tradition of the mediæval bestiary having passed away, the Englishman began to pay animated Nature the compliment of his exact observation, and the habit has never left him. It may be a far cry from the diarist of the hedgerow or the zoological garden to the great mind which compares and sifts evidence until a new *De Rerum Natura* darwinizes us; but the minute labour is essential to the dynamic result. What is more impressive in all the constitution of man than his ability and then his enterprise of looking beyond his own immediate affairs? The romance of discovery has not been confined to the Columbuses and the Keplers; it has twinkled in the track of many a humble local worthy with an eye for a bird or fish,

and it brightens the general seriousness of the kind
of naturalist who may be ridiculed by comic artists.
I cannot, for instance, deceive myself that the surface
of a work like Pennant's *History of Quadrupeds* (1781)
is not dry and corrugated. But beneath it there is a
regard for Nature's family which Pennant might claim
to be much more genuine a communion with the
spirit of the universe than the more ambitious reveries
of those who saw men as trees walking. There is
none of the mystic, or acting-mystic, in his descrip-
tions of animals' bodies and ways of life, but there
is a most satisfying sense that the better they are
known the better it must be for everybody. He
takes an artist's pleasure in perfecting his brief word-
portraits of his quadrupeds. He gazes at the black
bar in the middle of the hedgehog's spines with much
the same original gladness

> As when a mother does explore
> The rosemark on her long-lost child.

Long as it is, I must quote his curious eulogy of the
dog, point on point being driven home, agreeable
or disagreeable as it may be, until we have heard
a prose dithyramb on the way that Nature chose to
make this race. It is grim as truth, and as kind:

"The most faithful of animals: is the companion

of mankind: fawns at the approach of its master: will not suffer any one to strike him: runs before him in a journey; often passing backward and forward over the same ground: on coming to crossways, stops and looks back: very docile: will find out what is dropt: watchful by night: announces the coming of strangers: guards any goods committed to its charge: drives cattle home from the field: keeps herds and flocks within bounds: protects them from wild beasts: points out to the sportsman the game, by virtue of its acute sense of smelling: brings the birds that are shot to its master: will turn a spit: at *Brussels* and in *Holland* draws little carts to the herb-market: in *Sibiria* draws a sledge with its master in it, or loaden with provisions: sits up and begs: when it has committed a theft, slinks away with its tail between its legs: eats enviously, with oblique eyes: is master among its fellows: enemy to beggars: attacks strangers without provocation: fond of licking wounds: cures the gout and cancers: howls at certain notes in music, and often urines on hearing them: bites at a stone flung at it: is sick at the approach of bad weather: gives itself a vomit by eating grass: is afflicted with tape-worms: spreads its madness: grows blind with age: driven as unclean from the houses of the *Mahometans*: yet the same people establish hospitals for them, and allow them a daily dole of food: eats flesh, carrion, farinaceous vegetables, not greens: fond of rolling in carrion: dungs on a stone . . . . goes 63 days with young; brings from four to ten; the males like the dog, females like the bitch: its scent exquisite: goes obliquely: foams when hot, and hangs out its tongue: scarce sweats: about to lie down, often goes round the spot: its sleep attended with a quick sense of hearing: dreams."

Again leaving Pennant to stand as one instance of the English observers of animals with their own zeal and shrewdness of report, men glad to be alive in the same world with the whale and the elephant, I come to the ancient topic of the weather. On this topic much depends, and we are commonly reminded of it by our acquaintance, yet not in such vivacity of phrase as to thrill us with sympathy. The life of man, however, is still in the main connected by many invisible bonds with this same weather; Nature cannot do without it; in the sky she persists in her pageantry and her moods, and at times must be suspected of drenching man and beast all day with the object of art for art's sake when the sunset burns through the clouds. There have been, and there may remain, many persons in this country who

passed beyond the stage of adverse criticism of
Nature in this matter, and had delight and wonder
in watching the face of the sky, and skill in sketching
with words the changes of that changeless countenance.   Perhaps one must admit that the price of
wheat or barley mingled with the serenity of contemplation, but the effect as one may find it in print
is nevertheless beautiful, refreshing, and instructive
in the art of living in the world.   It is the touch of
Shelley in the ordinary man or woman.   A phrase
or two from the *Gentleman's Magazine* meteoro-
logical diaries in the days when Wordsworth was
emerging above the poetical horizon will yield the
distinctness of sensation with which "the weather"
may be chronicled: "May 19, White veil upon the
blue"; "November 10, Obscure, delightful day."
This kind of perception becomes with such a man
as William Gilpin a love-affair with sun and shower,
and through volume after volume you see this
exemplary parson watching the celestial painter, and
with pen and pencil too transcribing some fragment
of the aerial work, happy beyond measure when a
sunbeam darts its instant glory on a sail or a gull's
wing against the titan blackness of tempest.

The many Tours that were published in the days
of George the Third may introduce the subject of

guide-books, from the mention of which and the conventional imbecility or utilitarianism of modern examples no great addition to the central theme of the Englishman's feeling for Nature might be anticipated. Yet many of them have been primarily brought into existence by the simple and unhurried devotion of those who sought nothing better than their favourite ten square miles of Nature. Those ten square miles indeed, almost anywhere in England outside the tyranny of streets and streets and then streets, could furnish volumes of variety. A tithe map might be the plan of a master-work in human and natural harmonies; we have had White's *Selborne*. Mr H. M. Tomlinson sitting beside the little jetty of a fishing village can summon up the genii where most of us hear the water irrelevantly lapping the idle stones. But I am drifting away from my proposition that the earlier guide-books often embodied the typical English liking (to use no more ambitious term) for the wind on the heath. Sometimes unusually gifted writers have been moved to undertake the mechanical problem of a practical guide-book, in order to share their delight in their haunts with the public. I have in my hand, not Wordsworth's *Guide to the Lakes*, since Wordsworth and Nature have appeared together on the lecturer's platform sufficiently often, but Harriet Martineau's. The preface illustrates the English resolution not to wear the heart on the sleeve where any romantic vision of Nature may be suspected; she thanks the publisher and illustrators, and concludes, "We have all done our best to set forth a true presentment of a land we love, in the hope of inducing and enabling those who live in town or plain to know and love it as we do. If any think that we have painted it too fair, and that we love it fanatically, let them come and see."

So she begins, but as she makes her way forward with her remarkable, though directory-laden book, she gives away a secret or two; not fanatical rhapsodies, nor those superconscious appeals of Emily Brontë, but proofs of a nature-worship that "stands the test of every light." I do not imagine, in spite of Miss Bosanquet's recent book on Miss Martineau, that many readers have looked for triumphs of atmosphere, tone, and spirit in this or any other guide-book; I therefore choose a page or two which, were not English literature as wealthy as it is, would be considered essential reading. She is revealing mountain solitude. She presently finds its best symbol. "Perhaps a heavy buzzard may rise, flapping, from its nest on the moor, or pounce from a crag in the direction of any water-birds that may be about the springs and pools in the hills. There is no other sound, unless it be the hum of the gnats in the hot sunshine. There is an aged man in the district, however, who hears more than this, and sees more than people below would, perhaps, imagine. An old shepherd has the charge of four rain gauges which are set up on four ridges—desolate, misty spots, sometimes below and often above the clouds. He visits each once a month, and notes down what these gauges record; and when the tall old man, with his staff, passes out of sight into the cloud, or among the cresting rocks, it is a striking thought that science has set up a tabernacle in these wildernesses, and found a priest among the shepherds. That old man has seen and heard wonderful things—has trod upon rainbows, and been waited upon by a dim retinue of spectral mists. He has seen the hail and the lightnings go forth as from under his hand, and has stood in the sunshine, listening to the thunder growling, and the tempest bursting beneath his feet. He well knows the silence of the hills, and all the solemn ways in which that silence is broken. The stranger, however, coming hither on a calm sunny day may well fancy that a silence like this can never be broken."

Presently our guide speaks of the perpetual energy and design of Nature, and it is a confession of faith: "As for the material changes,—those wrought in silence by Nature are of the same quiet, gradual, inevitable kind that have been going on ever since the mountains were upreared. She disintegrates the rocks, and now and then sends down masses thundering along the ravines, to bridge over a chasm, or make a new islet in a pool. She sows her seeds in crevices, or on little projections, so that the bare face of the precipice becomes feathered with the rowan and the birch: and thus, ere long, motion is produced by the passing winds, in a scene where all once appeared rigid as a mine. She draws her carpet of verdure gradually up the bare slopes, where she has deposited earth to sustain the vegetation. She is for ever covering with her exquisite mosses and ferns every spot which has been left unsightly, till nothing appears that can offend the human eye, within a whole circle of hills. She even silently rebukes and repairs the false taste of uneducated man. If he makes his dwelling of too glaring a white, she tempers it with weather-stains: if he indolently leaves the stone walls and blue slates unrelieved by any neighbouring vegetation, she supplies the needful screen by bringing out tufts of delicate fern in the crevices, and springing coppice on the nearest slopes." This passage continues and is ended with the picture of new tarns glittering for the wild swans to light upon; the whole thing being an unquestioning adoration, without that vibrating mystical intuition which some have known—in short, the fullness of the normal English response to the mystery of things occurs here, in a guide-book.

The glad identification of a man's self with the life and business of the other tenants of this earth may be found in English books without a moment's difficulty. When Keats wrote that he could peck with the sparrow in the gravel, he was expressing the intuition of a genius, but others without that ray of light have been able to achieve the same ambition by devoted use and excellence of personality. If Bewick has any meaning, it is that of a world in which the dog, the plover, the farmer's wife, the tramp, the old pollard are all personalities to be watched and interpreted without bias in favour of the human species. If we set Bewick aside as being exceptional, and in any case as being more expressive in his engravings than his prose notes, we may still gather instances of this English power, which Marvell has depicted in some of his verdant tints; not quite

Annihilating all that's made
To a green thought in a green shade,

but at least "behaving as the wind behaves," and
seeing life as a fish or a moth might do.   There is an
inexhaustible supply of sympathetic description like
the following account of the "Disappointment of the
Cattle" when they come to their pool on a winter's
day:

> Sunk in the vale, whose concave depth receives
> The waters draining from these shelvy banks
> When the shower beats, yon pool with pallid gleam
> Betrays its icy covering.   From the glades
> Issuing in pensive files, and moving slow,
> The cattle, all unwitting of the change,
> To quench their customary thirst advance.
> With wondering stare and fruitless search they trace
> The solid margin: now bend low their heads
> In act to drink; now with fastidious nose
> Snuffing the marble floor, and breathing loud,
> From the cold touch withdraw.   Awhile they stand
> In disappointment mute; with ponderous feet
> Then bruise the surface: from the wood rebounds
> Each stroke, forth gushes the imprisoned wave.

I am not concerned with the art of writing in that
single example from the many in Gisborne's *Walks
in A Forest*, published the year Keats was born,
though I think it thorough; my meaning is that the

parson-poet is one of the disappointed herd, and
without any awkwardness he proceeds to compare
with this winter experience of his country companions the Arctic miseries of the English endeav-
ouring to discover the north-east passage to China.
As I think of this version of liberty, equality, frater-
nity, I am reminded of a stupid critical convention,
which only recognises "pompous diction" in the
old-fashioned phrases of natural observers—such as
"the plumy people," the "airy nations," the "bleat-
ing kind." These may not be masterpieces of style,
but they arise from a kindliness of soul which will
not be content with a dehumanised label. Between
friends there should be delicacy of spirit. The
degrees and ranks of natural history cannot preclude
that. "My dog and I," says the shepherd, "are
both grown old." Sometimes the Englishman will
proceed along this path of natural comprehension to
a point of (what is called) eccentricity. The Charles
Watertons and Frank Bucklands are comparatively
familiar representatives of this spiritual socialism
in Nature. But I may for the moment illustrate
my impressions with an agreeable gentleman whose
name I cannot find; and that, too, stamps the
modesty of the traditional attitude towards Nature
in this country. Anonymity, or a humorous pen-

name, goes with the self-denial which enables man to go out into new highways and see his real country-cousins.

My author is content to call himself "Acheta Domestica"; he produced, about the time of the Great Exhibition, a set of volumes called *Episodes of Insect Life*, published by Reeve and Benham. (Honoured names, vieing in this kind of excellence with John van Voorst; but the temptation to smuggle in a eulogy of publishers of books on Nature must be resisted.)   The *Episodes* make a book which, from the standpoint of a peaceful patriot, I would as soon possess as the original edition of *In Memoriam*. The author's method is exactly displayed in the elaborate cover-design; it shows a bower of grasses, twigs, and sprays of leaves, surmounted with a spider's web, and tenanted by spider, dragon-fly, ladybird, bee, stag-beetle, grasshopper, caterpillar, butterfly, moth; while in the midst on a little tree-stump sits the author, with opened book, dressed in knee-breeches and long-tailed coat and bands, his head like that of an insect with long antennæ, his pointing hand like the hand of a bee.   Then he proceeds with his zoological humanities throughout the year, inventing stories to make his observation ride easier, and accompanying his prose and verse with a series of beautiful coloured portraits of his friends the insects, and of caricatures and caprices to save us from any fear that he has lost touch with mankind.   It will still be said, perhaps, This is an admirable enthusiasm, but what of its effect as literature?   I answer that in any other country than one like ours, so "rich beyond the dreams of avarice" in splendid prose and verse, a pen like Acheta Domestica's would be considered something to crow about, and I will quote him in his normal eloquence. "Amongst the most beautifully painted of the cater-pillar race are those from which spring the elegant and distinguished tribe of Hawk-moths, known also as *Sphinxes*, from the form and attitudes, elsewhere described, of these their no less distinguished larvæ. None, perhaps, among them are more tastefully decorated than that of the 'privet,' with his doublet of the most brilliant apple-green laced by oblique stripes of white and purple, further adorned along the sides by orange-circled spiracles or breathing-holes, and finished at the nether end by a black and yellow horn.   Little inferior as respects colour is the garb of the Privet's cousin of the lime-tree.   His surtout also is of green, subdued towards the sides, but on the back so vivid as to dim by comparison the brightness of the newest leaves which open round him. His pervading hue is usually variegated on each side by seven oblique stripes of yellowish-white and crimson; his small mitre-shaped head is edged with white, and his six claws are tinged, like the tips of Aurora's fingers, with rosy red. His horn, or tail, is bright blue, and the whole surface of his body is dotted with regular rows of small tubercles, giving to the skin the appearance of shagreen. A granulated skin of this description is a common characteristic of hawk-moth caterpillars, though not confined entirely to their tribe. Have we, or have we not, described already that harlequin for variety of hues, and Grimaldi for grotesqueness, the caterpillar of the puss-moth?" But for that he turns to Izaak Walton, who does not outdo him in aptitude of metaphor.

The obscurity of men like this is due to their number. There is another class of evidence on the Englishman's delight in Nature, which is chiefly overlooked because it is so frequent. Who does not know the nineteenth-century gift-book with its supergilt covers and edges, the flowery frame round its pages, its long passages from Kirke White side by side with Shelley without any hesitation over pure poetry or critical guidance, its generous profusion of large and small engravings of the English scene?

These unwieldy and ill-bound books may not be
passed over without a thought of the character which
they reveal, the spirit which produced them and the
spirit which received them. They embody the
country's love of Nature, and are remarkable whether
we think of the multitude of writers whose inspiration supplied their pages, of the compilers and artists
whose willing toil embellished the selections, of the
unsophisticated men and women who liked to have
them because they valued the world they lived in.
Nothing could excel the sweetness of that Victorian
concord. Is this the nation of shopkeepers, that
in the full roar of industrial improvement desires
nothing more than an imaginative saunter with
William Collins and Samuel Palmer, with Thomas
Hood and Harrison Weir? Among those neglected
and faded books, there are some which give a fairly
wide view of our nature-poetry, though to present
its panorama would require a whole library. I would
name, as the type of these significant anthologies,
one that appeared in 1865, without any name on the
title page—*The Voices of the Year; containing the
Choicest Pastorals in our Language.* In its five
hundred double-columned pages we meet with many
of the aspects under which our poets have made
themselves and their listeners happy, at all seasons of

our Northern year; "prime old Tusser" gives his
rules, Milton his day-dreams, Vaughan his morning
call, Pope his leisure among the senatorial oaks, and
Coleridge his mountain hymn. When a man has
captured the notice of posterity by his own special
sunbeam of understanding, then his countrymen
must have some notion of his life; he is "made one
with Nature"; and so, in the simple work which I
am noticing, we have pictures, such as "View of
Hagley Park, the Residence of Lord Lyttelton, and
Frequently the Abode of Thomson," or, "View of
the Cottage of Shenstone's Schoolmistress, at Hales-
Owen, Shropshire, where Shenstone received the
Rudiments of his Education." That appreciation
leads duly to the numerous volumes of *Homes and
Haunts*—I should like to own them all—wherein the
voice of Nature from the woods, the hills and "swell-
ing floods" has spoken through poets to quiet
explorers and worshippers, and set them on an intention worthy of being described in the affecting elegy
of Dr Bridges:

> I love all beauteous things,
>   I seek and adore them;
> God has no worthier praise
> And man in his hasty days
>   Is honoured for them.

I too will something make
And joy in the making;
Although to-morrow it may seem
Like the empty words of a dream
Remembered on waking.

Give the Englishman good excuse, and he will rise above that reserve of his, and confess his true temper. It may be that he is bound by the laws of his making to begin as prosaically as is possible, but once he begins he works on quietly into some more vivid and independent and charming self-expression, and it is not rash to say that usually his highest ease is when he is alone in and with Nature. I am not in the least inclined to applaud any exploitation of that taste. "Nature" has been too often debased into a commercial opportunity, and the inner dream and desire of the citizen have been answered with false appearances in life, in literature, and in art. Ambition and necessity can turn anything to their purpose, and intellectual "substitutes" are not unknown; we have seen in our time a quantity of poems, for instance, which professed to take us out of our towns into the green wilderness, and to restore us from our roll-top desks to the "good brown earth." I am incapable of hearing any nature-poet who addresses me as "brother" in the wake of George Borrow, who batters me with a refrain of uncouth place-names, or who gives flower-names and no additions, without suspicion. I see breakers ahead when I am promised new and thrilling sensations in the serialised tragedy of a bream's private life. I am not wholly certain that I would rank Richard Jefferies' *Story of My Heart* beside Miller on *Gardening* for the truth about our intercourse with Nature. From heartiness without particularity, particularity without experience, and mysticism without plainness, an old faith debars me; it is the faith in the good sense of the Englishman. Where he is on ground meant for him, he advances without embarrassment or advertisement. The best of him is unknown until he has done it, and that, as was hinted, as a rule, requires some indirect opportunity. Only a "professional poet" will celebrate without some stratagem a beautiful experience of Nature; the "plain man" prefers a camera and a single epithet; but the plain man will sometimes make his meaning more complete. When that time comes, he probably adds something of value to the literature of his country, something that will never be famous but will be discovered with the peculiar respect due to what is genuine, and hidden.

If I may be indulged once more in the habit of

defending the claim of some parts of the English library to be represented in the history of our literature, as far as my subject is concerned, let me allude to the delightful and discursive kindness for "opening the window on Nature" which our dramatists have felt. With a Shakespeare all things were possible, and I will not call together my illustrations from his plays; they may linger in the background, while a more restricted, more citified age, the eighteenth century, discovers how constant is our turning to the country-green. The tragedy of "Douglas," long remembered as the environment of the notorious Norval, introduces the music of Nature as a charm:

> This is the place, the centre of the grove;
> Here stands the oak, the monarch of the wood.
> How sweet and solemn is this midnight scene!
> The silver moon, unclouded, holds her way
> Through skies where I could count each little star.
> The river, rushing o'er its pebbled bed,
> Imposes silence with a stilly sound.

Thomson, again, is not only a nature-painter in his poetical works; his dramas variously appeal to our sensibility for the life beyond our daily track. In his "Agamemnon," for instance, we must feel the brooding of an elemental presence over Troy:

> The night was dark and still; a heavier gloom
> Ne'er cover'd earth: in louring clouds the stars
> Were muffled deep; and not one ray below
> O'er all Mycenæ glimmer'd, or around it:
> When straight, at farthest east, a ruddy light
> Sprang up, and wide-increasing roll'd along,
> By turns diminish'd, and by turns renew'd,
> A wave of fire. At last it flamed, confess'd,
> From isle to isle, and beachy point to point,
> Till the last blaze at Nauplia ended plain.

That is spectacular and haunted Nature; but of Nature the friend the same play sings the praise. A character is marooned like Crusoe, and in course of time makes his misery his home:

> I ate my lonely meal without a tear,
> Nor sigh'd to see the dreadful night descend.
> In my own breast, a world within myself;
> In streams, in groves, in sunny hill and shade;
> In all that blooms with vegetable life,
> Or joys with kindred animal sensation;
> In the full-peopled round of azure heaven;
> Where'er I studious look'd, I found companions.

These passages may be enough, chosen from the myriad, to show how far we must pursue our inquiries if we would exactly view and review the nature-writings of England.

The word "joys" in the last extract brings one

within prospect of the distinction of those constel-
lated interpreters of Nature who are so often handed
about in a parcel labelled "The Romantic Movement." In Blake, in Wordsworth, in Coleridge, in
Shelley, in Keats, in Clare the spirit of Nature is a
universal glittering and animation, which may well
be called joy, even when it makes no discernible effect
of merriment or philosophic happiness. Now at
length there is a glory in the gliding trout, the soaring
lark, the sounding cataract, and the mind of man,
which in its instant reference to all the influences
of Nature transcends any other way of communica-
tion. The pleasures that the poet-farmer took in
his flock, the sportsman in his horse and hounds, the
wanderer in his cloud-colours and rock-masses, the
entomologist in his ants and bees, the gardener in
his calendar of fragrances and radiances, were all
leading to this lyrical wisdom. Without these new
writers, it is probable that the tribute of Washington
Irving to the English poetry of Nature would have
still been wholly just: "The pastoral writers of
other countries appear as if they had paid Nature an
occasional visit, and become acquainted with her
general charms; but the British poets have lived
and revelled with her,—they have wooed her in her
most secret haunts,—they have watched her minutest

caprices. A spray could not tremble in the breeze
—a leaf could not rustle to the ground—a diamond
drop could not patter in the stream—a fragrance
could not exhale from the humble violet, nor a daisy
unfold its crimson tints to the morning, but it has
been noticed by these impassioned and delicate
observers, and wrought up into some beautiful
morality." True, but with the advent of Coleridge
and Shelley the range of perception seems increased;
it is now no question merely of a breeze in the
willows, but of a spirit-wind "that rolls through all
things," of vibrations and impulses that move the
abysses of conscience, of a morality crowning all
moralities—that of

> The Light whose smile kindles the Universe,
> That Beauty in which all things work and move,
> That Benediction which the eclipsing Curse
> Of birth can quench not, that sustaining Love
> Which through the web of being blindly wove
> By man and beast and earth and air and sea,
> Burns bright or dim, as each are mirrors of
> The fire for which all thirst.

Distant as the Romantic heights might seem from
the country gentleman measuring his rainfall, the
clergyman preaching on the marvels of natural
phenomena, and the traveller approaching the twi-

light hill with the solemnity of a pilgrim, they were not disconnected from those; the preparation of centuries, the co-ordination of many observations and intuitions, came duly to their harvest in the new myth of a fair-destinied universe which man should know as proudly and gladly as now he knew the primrose and the linnet.

II

THE SPIRIT WOOED

Collins, Keats, Clare

If aught of oaten stop, or pastoral song,
May hope, chaste Eve, to soothe thy modest ear
  Like thy own solemn springs,
  Thy springs, and dying gales . . .

IF anything of country experience or studious guess
may not be counted mere intrusion, I come to repeat
some favourite masterpieces of English nature-poetry
and to indulge some trains of thought which they
have suggested, and I begin with one which has for
more than twenty years amazed and sustained me,
the "Ode to Evening," by William Collins. So far
as is known, it first appeared in the volume which he
published at the end of 1746, when he was twenty-
five years old—a time of wars and menaces and sacri-
fice, which Collins saw at first hand and interpreted
in his hymns and elegies. England was for him a
goddess, the mother of heroes; but better than that,
and for a longer age, she was the bride of peace and
the friend of Nature animate and inanimate. It is

as the sincerest of patriots, and devoutest of nature-suppliants, that Collins utters the mysterious orison which is remarked as his greatest poem.

For the original and local habitation of Nature in this poem there is no minute identifying evidence; but we may take the liberty of combining the districts of Winchester and Chichester, the South Downs and villages like "humble Harting," as the main ground of Collins's fancy. Here too Gilbert White found the same mood, and even wandered from his customary prose, with its seemingly responsive aptitude for a theme so delicate, into verses. But Collins, copiously brilliant in the various effects of verses, could not rest content with the usual sound of rhyme in the presence of his "nymph reserved"; and by a stroke of genius he chose the unrhymed form which Milton, whose artistry he fed upon with the appetite of sufficing originality, had somewhat stiffly practised. "Now teach me," Collins writes,

> Now teach me, maid composed,
> To breathe some softened strain;

that strain being the rhymeless stanza which he employs. Rhymeless, we call it; but, as evening is haunted with rumours and echoes of the quietened day, so the idyll of Collins is musical with a series of subdued and sometimes remotely set rhymes and assonances. Continuing the quotation just made, we instantly find an example, of which the purpose is clear—the exclamation of joy on the part of the man seeing the deity come to earth:

> Whose numbers, stealing through thy darkening *vale*,
> May not unseemly with its stillness suit,
>> As, musing slow, I *hail*
>> Thy genial loved return!

And that concluding word is a quiet consummation of a concluding note, the "small but sullen *horn*," two stanzas earlier. Presently we come to the vesper-bell, and then again there is in the verse a playing on sound which without superficial emphasis makes us live in the moment.

Such is the versecraft of the poem, intently and wholly communicating with the genius of time and place, and comparable for this with the hermit-hues of old Chinese paintings of grove and moon and symbolical wild-bird. I turn to the general form of the Ode. The first five stanzas are a conjuration and a petition to Evening, of an exquisite modesty yet resolve of imagination; by all her own beauties the poet requires her to smile on his verse. In the course of this, by choice of image and secret allusion, he hints how his great predecessors among the English poets have wooed and won the Spirit of his dream. The next two stanzas are a confession of his longing for Evening as the season when the fairy side of life holds the upper hand, when solitude resumes her sovereignty, and when all his being seeks no higher achievement than to wander like elf or nymph in the early starlight and dew. From this, the poet passes to three stanzas remembering those scenes which most delight him in these pilgrimages; the ruin by the lake, the field at rest from harvest, the hut on the hill with its window opening on a whole countryside stealing into sleep, and the vision of the divine dreamer over all, whose

> dewy fingers draw
> The gradual dusky veil.

And there he pauses, lingering as the last words compel us to linger. The subject has "wrought a silence," and expression has travelled into the inexpressible. When he begins afresh, it is in a different tone, to conclude the poem with an epilogue of three stanzas; in which he makes his vow, on behalf of all "holy and humble men of heart," through all the seasons and their changeful masque to keep the wonder, the grace, the modesty, and the kindness of Evening always before him.

I now return to the opening of the poem and to occasional notices of its beauties throughout; making at once this proviso, that I do not pretend to come near exhausting this fountain of allusion and significance. The better the reader of men like Shelley and Collins and Milton, the better the poetry; the fuller our recollection of nature, art, and literature, the more beautiful and pleasing the harmony of the work. It was pointed out in the *London Magazine* for 1821 that Collins is a re-creator of previous literature, in which he was profoundly capable, not so much by the renewed phrase but by the emotion borne on with his life. Through such imagery as at once declares the actual and intimates the intellectual, he contrives in his induction of the "Ode to Evening" to approach his subject and to honour those masters who had approached it already. The first line must recall young Milton in "Lycidas," and the bat's "short shrill shriek" is to be heard as though Spenser were standing beside the newcomer to this poetry. Presently the folding-star brings "Comus" into the region, and the "calm votaress" is of the same intuition. The elves who slept in flowers belong to the underwoods of Shakespeare, while they are also the perfumes and light airs that come from the bean or clover. "From the mountain's side" is another of Collins's communings with fair Fidele in the wilderness.

As with his literary reference and homage Collins is a master of courteous delicacy, so with his mythological touches he is sensitive to the finest point. Mere personification would construct, besides giving a statuesque coldness of impression, a style foreign to his English atmosphere; but the English mind in respect of Nature is sweetly compacted of direct and indirect associations, and the evening-star for us is still Hesperus as well. Evening, as she appears in this Ode, is a country girl, a Fairy Queen, a priestess, a goddess, a ghost in the sky. The sun is a "noble youth" from the Homeric legend, Phœbus Apollo; a knight, that must rest in his chivalric splendour. The bat and the beetle, rather than circumstances of natural history—though they certainly are such, and most accurately and rustically reported—are *dramatis personæ* and actors in the pageant of Vesper. The mists from the streams that cool the thirsty meadow are nymphs with coronals of sedge, fancies, yet things of the visible and sensuous world. The star is the gem of the heavens, the timekeeper of shepherd and sheep, the faithful emissary of evening ("*thy* folding-star") and the sprite who with his signal sets the other fairies at their task and ministry of peace.

But this quantity of circumstance must come to

an end. Underlying the whole fabric, the whole intricacy of decoration, there is the inspiration of the English alliance with and spiritual perfection in Nature. Even in hours of wild weather, there is the comfort, there the "prototype of rest," the secret immortality in whose tide we are all swayed and by whose waters we are purified and saved; the watcher and the humanities and solitudes which he contemplates are all subjects of that "quiet rule." That is the culmination of Collins's "Ode to Evening" and the cause why of all the charms in this incantation our country repeats most often and with the utmost understanding those lines,

> Be mine the hut
> That from the mountain's side
> Views wilds, and swelling floods,

> And hamlets brown, and dim-discovered spires,
> And hears their simple bell, and marks o'er all
> Thy dewy fingers draw
> The gradual dusky veil.

If it was the landscape round Winchester which principally reflected itself in that mirror of Collins, the transition to my next poetical pleasure cannot be hard; for Keats's "To Autumn," which, I believe, was the latest of his Odes, was inspired by a Sunday walk among the stubble-fields near Winchester.

Besides, like Collins, Keats was a poet of great comprehension within a little space, bringing together his enjoyments and impressions from the whole range of his experience, and with the young fearlessness of candid strength weaving into his arras all the colours that could be won from his mental and his physical use of life.   Like that of Collins, his style, on account of his rich resources and tragically necessary haste, is prone to obscurities and inequalities; such enthusiasts

> Cram their rich thievery up, they know not how.

"To Autumn" is scarcely a perfect poem, the touches of detail being a little blurred in repetition once or twice.   The "cool gleam" of the final work of art, I dare say, is disturbed by the iteration of the word "fruit," twice within the first six lines, when the general cornucopia of the season has been painted at once and for good in the powerfully ordered opening apostrophe:

> Season of mists and mellow fruitfulness.

A similar indistinctness of sense is caused by the halting repetition of the adjective "soft" ("soft-lifted," "soft-dying," "treble soft") in the last two stanzas.   This redundancy is a failing of which Keats himself was a convinced enemy, and opposed to his theory of the imagination "picked up and sorted to a pip." Also, perhaps, he had no special reason for the slight clash of sounds, within his rhymed form, which may be heard in "To *swell* the gourd and plump the hazel *shells*," "on a half-*reap'd* furrow sound *asleep*," "*Steady* thy laden *head*." This said, my complaints are over, and I take up the topic of the excellences and confluences of this beautiful poem.

The outline of the poem is not dissimilar to that of Collins's "Evening." The first stanza is an invocation, and of course a portraiture with the invocation. The second is a more personal idyll of adventures in the charmed country of this votaress, and at the close of this we are held by the spell of the verse as the poet and his allegorical spirit are held,

> Watching the last oozings, hours by hours.

The pause is ended and the poem resumed in a fresh motive by the question with which the third stanza opens,

> Where are the songs of Spring?

But that is only a means to an end; to give the poet his cue for a clear and unqualified vow of his true love for this goddess. "Think not of them." The succeeding music is all that he desires, and seems in its perfect innocence and "treble soft" and "wailful choir" as though it too could never cease; and it cannot. "So long, sure-found" (the bond of Collins) seems echoing in this same quiet permanence.

Mingling with the influences of the season, as Keats composes his Ode, are the presences of his older poets. A discarded reading certifies, what the general air of the piece suggests, that Chatterton's minstrel-song on Autumn is not forgotten—

> When Autumn sere and sunburnt doth appear
> With his gold hand gilding the fallen leaf.

The rosy reflection on the stubble-plains seems congenial with that gleam from Collins's "upland fallows grey." The closing lines afford a glimpse into the "Autumn" of James Thomson; the pageant-figure of Autumn is in the manner of Spenser, particularly in that march of the months and seasons in the "Two Cantos of Mutabilitie." Of the personifications and imaginative animations in the Ode, no praise could be too high; like Collins, Keats makes no imports of cold sculpture. Clare indeed complained that he favoured the classical legend overmuch—that he "saw behind every rose-bush a thrumming Apollo"; but Clare was especially happy with the "Ode to Autumn," and among his

papers are some transcripts from it. The spirit-form
of Autumn is made remote and near by a series of
manifestations like those of Evening in Collins, or in
a pretty lyric on Solitude by Thomson—

> A thousand shapes you wear with ease,
> And still in every shape you please.
> Now wrapt in some mysterious dream,
> A lone philosopher you seem;
> Now quick from hill to vale you fly,
> And now you sweep the vaulted sky;
> A shepherd next you haunt the plain
> And warble forth your oaten strain.

The Season of Keats is a rural, agricultural, bee-
keeping Genius, a wise worthy of Hampshire; then
a gipsy in a barn, cool and still sunny; a dozing
reaper; a gleaner poising along the stepping-stones;
a ghost of the farm, watching on through many
cider-makings; and then, too, a fairy queen with
her little musicians, a power of beauty ordaining
the sad tranquillity of sky and sunset. In this last
estimate, the figures of gnats, and lambs, and crickets,
and robin and swallows, "still to Nature true," are
heightened by the imagination into the personages
proper to the majesty of the central person; the
whole wide earth and sweep of sky are filled with
their moods and melodies. Autumn withdraws with

them into the distance, but they shine and sing in that temperate lucidity with clear pre-eminence.

I now submit some observations on the details of word and phrase here and there. The first stanza, being an address to the season, has been wrongly supplied by the compositor with a full stop at the end, but it does not cease in that point; the main sense of the long sentence is in the question following. Autumn . . ., who hath not seen thee? How friendly is that word "conspire"! and how rich in country understanding; as is the noun "cottage-trees," picturing the sort which on their crooked, chopped, propped limbs support the drying linen or the swinging children. There too is the friendliness of England felt. As the stanza proceeds, the conspiring country gods create a superabundance of benevolence; clause is added to clause by the poet, bee-fashion, "more and still more," in the opulence of the season. The stanza, like the honeycomb, is "o'er-brimmed," and the crowded sentence ends in the one succeeding. In that, "whoever seeks abroad" can find a likeness for Autumn, poet or no poet, since pleasure and plenty are the most human of topics, and this season is the favourite. The "fume" of poppies is a splendid simplicity, with its dual notion of perfume and an opiate. The gleaner is another ancient earth-child, and if we have not realised the old glory of country life from the preceding symbols of barn-floor and sickle, we do so now, and the story of Ruth is in the English corn. In the last stanza, there is a rich unity between the sky bloomed with its clouds and the thought of the fruit of the earth bloomed with its blue veils; the conspiracy of blessing is now matured to a serene entirety of natural richness. In case Keats is thought to refer in contradictory manner to Spring with his "Then," it may be noted that the adverb is not in antithesis to "and now"; it means "moreover." One little local word is often misinterpreted here, too; "hilly bourn," I should say, is not an allusion to Lear's "chalky bourn," but rather to Hampshire, as in the name of Selborne, and may be pleasantly considered as Keats's glance of friendliness to the friendly countryside which helped him to his poem; which dissolved away for a time the traces of his life's contests and sad apprehensions, and united him with the equipoise and still splendour of Nature in autumn.

A third nature-poem now calls for our regard, one which is on the subject of Keats's Ode and in the unrhymed stanza of Collins. This is the "Autumn"

of John Clare, in some lights the best poet of Nature
that this country and for all I know any other
country ever produced. Clare was known in his
time as the Northamptonshire Peasant Poet, and is,
I am afraid, still looked upon as such by many of
those who have heard of him. Simple as he may at
a hasty reckoning appear, he is not so when he is
known better: Clare is a rustic, but imaginative
enough to see the meaning of that; he is an exact
naturalist, but a poet of the mystical temper as well;
he is not learned, but makes considerable excursions
into learning, by which he is enabled not to stand
still between naivety and great art, and can be at
home in both. There is extraordinary development
in his poetry between the early clownish scrawl of
alehouse ballads and the later work of which the
Dantesque "I am! but what I am none cares or
knows!" is the most generally reprinted. However,
this is not the place for attempting an analysis
of Clare's work; my eyes are on the poem
"Autumn," written at the time of his maturest
and least distracted powers, and certainly one
of the most sustained and creative of his pieces.
It first appeared, a little battered, in Cunningham's
Anniversary for 1829, and was collected in *The Rural
Muse*, 1835:

> Syren of sullen moods and fading hues,
> Yet haply not incapable of joy,
>   Sweet Autumn! I thee hail
>   With welcome all unfeigned;
>
> And oft as morning from her lattice peeps
> To beckon up the sun, I seek with thee
>   To drink the dewy breath
>   Of fields left fragrant then . . .

So Clare begins.   His invocation of a spirit stranger in mien and characteristics than those of the other poets just mentioned is not long; in the third stanza it closes, and it is, he says, the end of Autumn that he intends to meditate.   Then comes a succession of pictures of solitude, such as he has particularly frequented in autumn; he pauses from these, and seems to confess that none of these will capture his desired supreme vision.   He again utters his desire—he invokes the answer of Nature:

> Sweet Vision, with the wild dishevelled hair,
> And raiment shadowy of each wind's embrace,
>   Fain would I win thine harp
>   To one accordant theme.

If only the mystery will take his verse as she takes the forest for her instrument! This is Clare's "Make me thy lyre."   He fancies her under the oak, a lover beside him, with him, looking out on

the disorder'd scenes of woods and fields,
Ploughed lands, thin travelled with half-hungry sheep,
Pastures tracked deep with cows,
Where small birds seek for seed;

on the herdboy pulling down the berries from the
thorn, and the hedger red-cheeked and hardy in the
dykeside, the mower with his stubbling-scythe,
the thatchers on barn and rick, and the "haunted
hare" started and scared into the woods. Then he
suddenly looks for his "wild sorceress" beside him,
and blesses her for her "restless mood," and "the
silence that is thine" in all this minor unrest; the
enigmatic moments when the din of joy is past, and
the storm is not come. But a change in the note of
the wind in the midst of this true and beautiful
melancholy warns him; even this dark-glorious
presence is doomed.

Now filtering winds thin winnow through the woods
In tremulous noise, that bids, at every breath,
Some sickly cankered leaf
Let go its hold and die.

And now the bickering storm, with sudden start,
In flirting fits of anger carps aloud,
Thee urging to thine end,
Sore wept by troubled skies.

Autumn, "disorderly divine," is going; the gold on
the leaf is the sign of her death—those dyes "prepare

her shroud." The queen of the winds, she droops beside him, and the dirge is low; the lark alone arises with his inexhaustible heart of music and goodwill, but then comes silence, and Autumn's grave. "That time is past." And yet, if the mystery has escaped, next year there will be a chance again for a song in her honour and to her liking: when she

> from her ivied trance
> Awakes to glories new.

The associations of Clare's "Autumn" with previous poetry are soon summed up; Collins has taught him a means of rendering a difficult music in Nature without rhyme, and given him a word or two, as "the willing lark" and the "faint and sullen brawl" of the stream. Shelley, of whom he knows a little, is with him in the "unpremeditated" song not of the lark but the child, and Keats in the "winnowing" wind. But the larger effect is that of a dweller in the woods, who is in love with what may or may not have been regarded as a symbol. Even Clare's "votaress" or "season" is a vision uncertain as those far-projected fluttering forms which some are said to see on the wind.

> The earth hath bubbles,

and she may be of them; it is not with him as with

Collins, who changes his picture of Evening with all the design of a mythological painter, or with Keats, who similarly enriches the canvas with a masque of gleaners, reapers, cider-makers. It is a direct though a pale passion, and can have at the end only one aim and expectation—a vision, apart from the creations of our normal affection and thought. Perhaps it will be reckoned fantastic to interpret Clare's "Autumn" in this almost psychic way, but a great part of his verse is a history of the transference of love in him from woman to Nature. He describes the poet as "a secret thing, a man in love none knoweth where"; he sums up his autobiography in lyrics of which the correct text has not been found, but which even in their injured state reveal the thrilling enigma of his heart. "I hid my love when young"—and then, the companionship of woman became more beautiful and immutable in a wood-change:

> I met her in the greenest dells
> Where dewdrops pearl the wood bluebells;
> The lost breeze kissed her bright blue eye,
> The bee kissed, and went singing by.
> A sunbeam found a passage there,
> A gold chain round her neck so fair;
> As secret as the wild bee's song
> She lay there all the summer long.

Having this Grace, this Dryad always in hope and almost in ocular proof, Clare wrote his poems as if for her; not all of them, but the later kind, when his old friends in London had died or drifted from him. He did not fail at times to regard verse as an art for the use of mankind, and indeed accomplished such examples of his intellectual eagerness as a series of poems in the manner of Elizabethan writers; but more and more he conceived his chief singing to be an offering to that mystery whom he loved, a repetition of all her endowments, her lineaments, her devotions and delights. So hastening on and giving her "his posies, all cropt in a sunny hour" with childlike haste and ecstasy, he did not shape his compositions in the intense school of Collins and Keats. They lose, in the arbitration of our criticism, for that reason, and the splendid "Autumn" which we are considering now is as a whole, as a marshalling of idea and circumstance, inferior to the other two Odes. But we can, by a sympathy of the imagination, approach Clare's poem in the light of his wooing of the "fair Flora," the wind-spirit, the music-maker, the shepherdess, and accept his unpremeditated and disunited perfections so. No one has surpassed these perfections in themselves, these tokens of his secret love. They may be classed as "observation," but only true passion can observe in Clare's way,

> By overshadowed ponds, in woody nooks,
> With ramping sallows lined, and crowding sedge,
>   Which woo the winds to play,
>   And with them dance for joy;
>
> And meadow pools, torn wide by lawless floods,
> Where water-lilies spread their oily leaves,
>   On which, as wont, the fly
>   Oft battens in the sun;
>
> Where leans the mossy willow half way o'er,
> On which the shepherd crawls astride to throw
>   His angle clear of weeds
>   That crowd the water's brim;
>
> Or crispy hills, and hollows scant of sward,
> Where step by step the patient lonely boy
>   Hath cut rude flights of stairs
>   To climb their steepy sides;
>
> Then track along their feet, grown hoarse with noise,
> The crawling brook, that ekes its weary speed,
>   And struggles through the weeds
>   With faint and sudden brawl.

You cannot reply "Notebook, notebook" to this exactitude, this close inventory of little things, of which Clare's work presents an infinity; it is the eye of a lover that feasts on such glances, gestures, and adornings of his mistress. Through all, her life gives life, her wonder gives wonder. The fly on the lily-leaf might have little meaning, did not that "sorceress" set him there, and what she does is to Clare touched with hieroglyphic eternity.

Hence, too, this happiness of animation, this familiar characterising of what are called "objects of landscape." All are equal here in the universal fancy of autumn. The sedge and the winds have their pastime apart like a group of children; the floods were common trespassers; the lonely boy and weary brook alike are patient in their labours of indolence. In the poem too there is another lonely boy, who exactly like the sedge "woos the winds" with his song. The lark springs up "to cheer the bankrupt pomp" of the time, and it is when the wind "bids" that the cankered leaf "lets go its hold"; in short, it is all one whether a ploughman passes or a bee. They bear the impress of the strange siren Autumn, and play their part without distinction of power and glory. I must not deaden this vitality of Clare's nature-vision with too much talking. He has commented on it himself in several poems, giving "every weed and blossom" an equality with whatever this world contains:

All tenants of an ancient place
　And heirs of noble heritage,
Coeval they with Adam's race
　And blest with more substantial age.
For when the world first saw the sun
　These little flowers beheld him too,
And when his love for earth begun
　They were the first his smiles to woo.

It is that last word, if one word can be, which is the keyword to John Clare's long life of unselfish, uncopied nature-poetry.

III

THE UNKNOWN GOD

H. Vaughan, Wordsworth, Coleridge, Shelley

From the *Natural Theology* of Paley to the *Parables of Nature* by Mrs Gatty, there repose the countless attempts of the English race to ascertain what divine scheme is concealed behind and within the appearances of our present surroundings, "to look" (one cannot evade the old and hard-worked quotation) "through Nature up to Nature's God." In clumsy hands this altogether creditable plan of persistence has become a painful disciplinary rod. Many of us have read *Father and Son*, and children have been harassed even by such good-natured men as Bunyan, who in his book of poems for them must spoil the spring by writing grim promises on rose-leaves:

> Thus Adam's race did bear this dainty rose,
> And doth the same to Adam's race expose.
> But those of Adam's race which at it catch,
> Them will the race of Adam claw and scratch.

With the best intentions, instead of opening Nature's book to us, some of our forefathers have shut it, and it is to be feared that the process continues, though possibly not so much in literature. Faith as it is prescribed among us too often assumes the form of a disgust with this fresh world about us; God created it, and it is well enough, but we must look past it to the crystal floor and Sun of Suns. The fear of paganism represses that joy of intuition which alone can give reasonable hope of "some more azure sky." The miracle of Easter has its evidences in every meadow at that bright day, but these seem to be regarded as scenery, worth general reference perhaps, but not in the same spirit of sublimer reassurance as is proper within the four walls of our Church.

Doubtless the question is one of individuality. Give one man a garden, and he will discover one kind of God in it, and throw the flowers on the rubbish-heap. Give another man a garden, and, like the celebrated author of the *Meditations among the Tombs*, he will do very well by the flowers— "Here, the *Hyacinth* hung her silken bells, or the Lilies reared their silver pyramids,"—but not so well by the Creator; "The whole was fitted up in the highest taste, and furnished with every pleasurable ornament. On purpose to harmonise with all that *lavish gaiety*, which seemed to smile over all the face of Nature. On purpose to correspond with that *vernal* delight, which came breathing on the wings of every fragrant gale. I may add, on purpose to remind the beholder of those *immortal mansions*, which are decorated with images infinitely more splendid, with objects unspeakably more glorious. Where Holy Beings will spend, not a few vacant hours in refined amusement, but a boundless eternity in the consummation of joy.—For to a well-turned mind, Nature is a preceptor; and these are her instructive lessons. To the pure in heart, even sense is edifying; and these are its delicate moralities." Put a Coleridge in the garden, and you receive a parable of Nature in honour of actuality and the soul of creation: "How beautiful a circumstance, the improvement of the flower, from the root up to that crown of its life and labours, that bridal-chamber of its beauty and its twofold love, the nuptial and the parental—the womb, the cradle, and the nursery of the garden!"

Among those who saw God walking in the garden without making others unhappy by applications of didactic insularity, that plain seventeenth-century churchman Henry Vaughan continues to answer my spiritual and realistic appeal. It is scarcely likely that his poems, which were for two centuries almost completely ignored, will ever become widely popular, but those who take to Vaughan at all are apt to make him their intimate friend. His great excellence is that, with full reverence for the modesty of Nature, he records some intuitions of his which anticipate those of Blake and of Wordsworth, and have a quiet certainty about them not found in Blake, and a primitive quality not allowed much room in the high and spacious intellectual architecture of Words-worth. Vaughan is a nature-poet comparable with Clare in his retired communings, but his secret is not that of sylvan or aerial romance; he is not in love with a shadowy goddess, half-woman, half-flower. He desires to speak with "his Creator, God"; a Being remoter than the stars, and nearer than the stones on his Welsh journey, a Source of life so com-plex and so simple that even those stones are mag-netic with him, and almost speak. The five senses, to Vaughan, are not things for scorn and disuse; but they are a "fleshy dress" which will not let him see Heaven immediately, or comprehend the conversation of God's creatures. And yet there are moments when

Some strange thoughts transcend his wonted themes,
     And into Glory peep.

The opening poem of *Silex Scintillans* discloses one of those moments; on a walk in spring, as he gazed on the primroses which were gazing at the sun, he heard

> A rushing wind
> Which still increas'd, but whence it stirred
> No where I could not find.
>
> I turned me round, and to each shade
> Dispatch'd an Eye,
> To see if any leafe had made
> Least motion or reply;
> But while I list'ning sought
> My mind to ease,
> By knowing where 'twas, or where not,
> It whisper'd: *Where I please.*

Here is that beauty which Keats has called "a little noiseless noise among the trees," suggested in natural circumstance, and prophetically felt and ascribed. This dual perception of Vaughan's is everywhere operative. The greater heaven does not blind him to the heaven less. Even his imperfection is confessed with such a sensitive innocence that the present is made celestial.

> Here of this mighty spring I found some rills
> With ecchoes beaten from th' eternall hills.
> Weak beames and fires flash'd to my sight
> Like a young East, or Moone-shine night.

What gives his verse such an attractive openness
is perhaps, above all, his love for light in all its change
and charm. He does not despise the earth beneath,
but it is in the air and the heavens that he holds his
finest conversation, and wins his liveliest colours and
tunes. At night he watches with those

> Fair ordered lights, whose motion without noise
>   Resembles those true joys
> Whose Spring is on that hill where you do grow
>   And we here taste sometimes below;

or the moonlight becomes so cloudless and pure that
he is again in prospect of a mystery—

> I saw Eternity the other night,
> Like a great Ring of pure and endless light,
>   All calm, as it was bright;
> And round beneath it, Time, in hours, days, years,
>   Driven by the spheres,
> Like a vast shadow moved, in which the world
>   And all her train were hurl'd.

While the night wears on, he hears the crowing cock,
and still it is the working of light that holds his
imagination; the community between the penthouse
and the great Original is his lamp.

> Father of lights! what sunnie seed,
>   What glance of day hast thou confined
> Into this bird?   To all the breed

> This busie ray thou hast assigned;
>   Their magnetisme works all night,
>   And dreams of Paradise and light.

At dawn he is for ever melodious on this same visitant happiness, and then particularly seems to know "the present deity" in the new-created stir and jubilee all round:

> Shall these early, fragrant hours
>   Unlock thy bowres?
> And with their blush of light descry
> Thy locks crown'd with eternitie?
> Indeed it is the only time
> That with thy glory doth best chime;
> All now are stirring, ev'ry field
>   Full hymns doth yield;
> The whole Creation shakes off night,
> And for thy shadow looks the light;
> Stars now vanish without number,
> Sleepie planets set and slumber,
> The pursie clouds disband and scatter,
> All expect some sudden matter;
> Not one beam triumphs, but from far
>   That morning-star.

When the full day has come, over Vaughan spreads out, and from earth is reflected, "the brightest day," the temper of which creates in his verse a singular fullness of tone and amplitude of movement—

Sweet, downie thoughts, soft Lily-shades, calm streams . . .

if there is cloud in his sky, then the rainbow rises
and whitens the black menace,

> Storms turn to Musick, clouds to smiles and air.

At evening he cannot be deserted by his genius for
light, and his hill is "drest in faint beams after the
sun's remove," in emanations and hauntings of the
glory of noon.

The meditation of Vaughan gives us a noble world
to live in, and worlds on worlds beyond that; his
sense of the panorama of Nature, although he never
adventures into elaborate and lengthy poems on the
subject, is supremely impressive. The astronomical
sublimity is in him, and he paints the sky as far and
lustrous as John Crome. This might be an excellence sufficient for one poet; but Vaughan conspicu-
ously achieves another. He is a quick, kind, and
personal illuminator of the humbler forms of Nature
and country life, and this homely affection brings his
greater visions within the reader's sympathy just as
though, plunged into some new bewildering cosmos,
a human hand touched us and a known voice remarked, "Well, old man, how's London looking?"
An instance of this familiar kinship in Vaughan is
his most famous line, already cited—

> I saw Eternity *the other night.*

But his quality is not comprised in a few passages. We accumulate it as we go, and discover his picture in a prospect of flowers little by little. His landscape is won by experience. Dark hills, swift streams, steep ways appear; mountains, with clear heights gleaming, and caves glooming; rough tracks with tumble-down cottages and shed-like inns; oak-woods, green shades, spring-wells, solitary stones, fallen trees and bushes; waterfalls and vapours, warm summer showers; the panniered ass and grazing cow; and "the loved physician" among his beehives and beds of herbs and flowers, violet and tulip and balm.

Of these local testimonies of Nature, that lyric on the Waterfall has been often and justly chosen as a fine example. It certainly proves Vaughan's instinct for leading thought heavenward not by contempt of this world's "masques and shadows," but by the best account of them which his poetical colours and tunes could arrive at.

> With what deep murmurs, through time's silent stealth,
> Doth thy transparent, cool, and watery wealth
>   Here flowing fall,
>   And chide, and call,
> As if his liquid, loose retinue staid
> Lingering, and were of this steep place afraid;
>   The common pass,
>   Where, clear as glass,

> All must descend
> Not to an end,
> But quicken'd by this deep and rocky grave,
> Rise to a longer course more bright and brave.

"Dear stream! dear bank," he proceeds, but without so definite a phrase we should have been sure of the love which he feels for a fellow-tenant of this time and space of ours; that alone could create in words so perfect a character of a water-spirit, could resyllable his voice and reflect his perennial beauty, even discover in him a sort of emotions. The poem, like most of Vaughan's, does not maintain itself to the close, towards which he moralises the matter, but even his fallings-off are vivid, and to the end we hear "this loud brook's incessant fall."

To pass to Wordsworth, although he was a reader of Vaughan, is on the whole to enter another world of poetry, and not in every mood can one be glad of the migration. Incomparably beyond Vaughan in mental survey and discrimination, in eloquence and the poet's art, in experience of crisis and character, Wordsworth does not always give us the impression of an eye that can detect what is hidden from common apprehensions as Vaughan does. After much learned talking, it was the voice of innocence which put an end to the case. But this is incidental;

we do not always choose a sonata before a madrigal, but we know where the grandeur lives. Vaughan would have been frightened by Wordsworth's charter of the poetic constitution—first, observation and description; secondly, sensibility; thirdly, reflection; fourthly, imagination and fancy; fifthly, invention; and lastly, judgment. He could scarcely have *classed* his poems. In the long run, perhaps even Wordsworth's classifications of the immortal works slide into one principal fact—they are naturepoems. I have before me the four-volume edition of 1820, by which date Wordsworth had nearly enough terminated his poetic existence, and it begins with a little piece very like Vaughan on the evening shower, which is not too ancient to come forth anew:

> My heart leaps up when I behold
>   A Rainbow in the sky:
> So was it when my life began;
> So is it now I am a Man;
> So be it when I shall grow old,
>   Or let me die!
> The Child is Father of the Man;
> And I could wish my days to be
> Bound each to each by natural piety.

They were. It is possible sometimes to mistake Wordsworth for the Creator rather than the created, and he has a tendency to give Nature a penny for her amusing prattle and tell her to run along now like a good girl. There is a slight interference of the comic with "Wordsworth upon Helvellyn!" There is a famous insipidity in the applied theory of elemental diction for natural topics:

> That is work of waste and ruin—
> Do as Charles and I are doing!

And yet in sum Wordsworth is himself a whole library of various poetry, descriptive and evocative and revelative of Nature.

In the matter of precise and full-tinted portraiture of Nature, Wordsworth disclosed himself—at least to the bright eye of Coleridge—so early as 1793, when he was twenty-one. If he had died after the publication of "The Evening Walk" and "Descriptive Sketches," he would have been remembered and resorted to as an extremely skilful and wide-eyed observer, with all the vocabulary that is necessary for communicating the attire and the action of a favourite scene.

> Sweet are the sounds that mingle from afar,
> Heard by calm lakes, as peeps the folding star,
> Where the duck dabbles 'mid the rustling sedge,
> And feeding pike starts from the water's edge,

> Or the swan stirs the reeds, his neck and bill
> Wetting, that drip upon the water still;
> And heron, as resounds the trodden shore,
> Shoots upward, darting his long neck before.

Even the alert Clare could scarcely have responded more eagerly to what was happening. One may be permitted a sigh that, in Wordsworth's later works, with easier course of expression there came a less vivid or instantaneous description. But in the discovery of deeper worlds, it was to be expected that a more exclusive mood would prevail over such brightness.

> That inward eye
> Which is the bliss of solitude

would choose its images according to its decisions; the receptive Wordsworth must change to the adjudicatory. "Lines composed a few miles above Tintern Abbey" in 1798, marked the development.

> Nature then
> (The coarser pleasures of my boyish days
> And their glad animal movements all gone by,)
> To me was all in all.—I cannot paint
> What then I was. The sounding cataract
> Haunted me like a passion; the tall rock,
> The mountain, and the deep and gloomy wood,
> Their colours and their forms, were then to me

An appetite: a feeling and a love,
That had no need of a remoter charm,
By thought supplied, or any interest
Unborrowed from the eye.—That time is past . . .

The ruralist gone, in his place appears the religious
theorist, a sadder and a wiser man, whose verse has
an expansive and stately command of things visible
and invisible, a solemn tidal irresistibility.

And I have felt
A presence that disturbs me with the joy
Of elevated thoughts; a sense sublime
Of something far more deeply interfused,
Whose dwelling is the light of setting suns,
And the round ocean and the living air,
And the blue sky, and in the mind of man:
A motion and a spirit, that impels
All thinking things, all objects of all thought,
And rolls through all things.

Now was Wordsworth a new, an English
Lucretius. The lesser part of him "broke loose" (as
his rustic neighbour said) in "Peter Bells" and other
verses made to support a critical proposition. There
were to be two voices from him, as the inspired
parodist declares; but we will not attend to the nois-
ings of the "old half-witted sheep." "The sea"
counts for more; it was the undertone of British
education and poetry, indeed of feeling towards

Nature, for a century, and still we travel on that Wordsworthian pomp of waters. After "Tintern Abbey" he could hardly sound a more lofty or profound note, but he increased its volume and accompanied it with a splendid system of related emotion and observation, hoping at last to complete a life-work illustrative in all its proportions of humanity in action with natural influences. He would depict, and show in his great design, the Nature which the old Cumberland beggar or leech-gatherer or cottage child knew, the Nature which the small celandine or the River Duddon knew, the Nature which shaped his powers of mind and supplied his life, the Nature which dominated the character of nations and the sleep of great cities. I cannot do justice in so meagre and exterior an abstract to that construction of poetry in which even the Sonnets were to be considered as side-chapels to the central glory. Where would the Ode, "Intimations of Immortality from Recollections of Early Childhood," be assigned by Wordsworth in this temple of the Muses? At all events, in the edition of 1820, from which the huge philosophic narrations are excluded, this Ode stands last, and Wordsworth means it to be his last word on his attitude to Nature, for he prefixes to it the following connexional quotation:

The Child is Father of the Man;
And I could wish my days to be
Bound each to each by natural piety.

See vol. i. p. 3.

In a manner, he had set out with the simple profundity of Henry Vaughan, and with that he finishes his course. All other intimations must "consign to this"—that in lucky moments an innocent mind can "see eternity" just over the hedge. Wordsworth protests that his own super-sense has been taken from him by reason of the very long journey, yet he travels back even in this vale-diction, and submits all subsequent conquest of human life to the excitement of the divine ambiguity: rejoicing not for "that which is most worthy" (a dull distinction),

But for those first affections,
Those shadowy recollections,
  Which, be they what they may,
Are yet the fountain light of all our day,
Are yet a master light of all our seeing;
  Uphold us—cherish—and have power to make
Our noisy years seem moments in the being
Of the eternal Silence: truths that wake,
    To perish never;
Which neither listlessness, nor mad endeavour,
    Nor Man nor Boy,

Nor all that is at enmity with joy,
Can utterly abolish or destroy!
  Hence, in a season of calm weather,
    Though inland far we be,
Our Souls have sight of that immortal sea
      Which brought us hither;
        Can in a moment travel thither,—
And see the Children sport upon the shore,
And hear the mighty waters rolling evermore.

Even in comparison with the view and insight of Wordsworth, the powers of Coleridge appear, in Wordsworth's adjective, "marvellous." There is no more commonly neglected author, the fault being partly that of Coleridge himself, who scribbled so much claptrap in verse in his early days, in prose often, and left us in a quicksand of half-begun work; partly of the editors. We have neither a complete edition, nor a broad selection. For the present argument I shall consider Coleridge through some of the poems and some of the almost more fascinating notes in his private notebooks, of which a number were printed in his *Literary Remains* and more by his studious and poetic grandson, the late Ernest Hartley Coleridge, in *Anima Poetæ*, 1895. Few people know this book, but it is crowded with startling reflections, beautiful word-pictures, and varied humanities. If anyone wishes to realise what F. T.

Palgrave says of Coleridge—"to take a figure from physical science, the union of Nature with the soul in him is chemical, not mechanical combination"— then *Anima Poetæ* is the swiftest intelligencer. But before I point out a few of its mysteries, I venture to annotate some of Coleridge's nature-poems. Of these, the principal group contains meditations in blank verse, not unlike that of Wordsworth, and verging on the same philosophic ground.

> Ah! slowly sink
> Behind the western ridge, thou glorious sun!
> Shine in the slant beams of the sinking orb,
> Ye purple heath-flowers! richlier burn, ye clouds!
> Live in the yellow light, ye distant groves!
> And kindle, thou blue ocean! So my friend
> Struck with deep joy may stand, as I have stood,
> Silent with swimming sense; yea, gazing round
> On the wide landscape, gaze till all doth seem
> Less gross than bodily; and of such hues
> As veil the Almighty Spirit, when he makes
> Spirits perceive his presence.

The famous and answered prayer for Hartley Coleridge is of the same import, although in S. T. Coleridge's expression the endless leaping of his mind into the psychology of everything makes the meaning a little less direct and potent than Wordsworth's:

> But thou, my babe! shalt wander like a breeze
> By lakes and sandy shores, beneath the crags
> Of ancient mountain, and beneath the clouds
> Which image in their bulk both lakes and shores
> And mountain crags: so shalt thou see and hear
> The lovely shapes and sounds intelligible
> Of that eternal language, which thy God
> Utters . . .

Yet we pause in Coleridgean fashion; this poet of all men might have seen God walking in the garden, might have heard "sounds of a strange kind," but would not believe the report of his own experience; must discover a psychological explanation.

In 1802 he has arrived at an explanation of the beauties and influences of Nature. He is not the first to work in that particular thought. "It goes so heavily with my disposition that this goodly frame, the earth, seems to me a sterile promontory; this most excellent canopy, the air, look you, this brave o'erhanging firmament, this majestical roof fretted with golden fire, why, it appears no other thing to me but a foul and pestilent congregation of vapours." Hamlet-Coleridge discovers that his sky is only a tint, some clouds, some stars, a crescent moon. "I gaze—and with how blank an eye!" In short, there is no cause in Nature apart which waits to surprise us into new glories.

> O Lady! we receive but what we give,
> And in our life alone does nature live.

That was the message of "Dejection." What
follows is commentary; he has heard voices, seen
landscapes of the finest charm, but

> Joy is the sweet voice, joy the luminous cloud;
>   We in ourselves rejoice!
> And thence flows all that charms or ear or sight,
>   All melodies the echoes of that voice,
> All colours a suffusion from that light.

Many years later, however, Coleridge is not so sure,
and he confesses it in a modest sonnet "To Nature":
"it may indeed be fantasy," he begins, but he has
fallen back at length on the chance that he may
receive what "all created things" may have to give.
He now proclaims that there exist sweet influences,
in the world of leaves and flowers.

> And if the wide world rings
> In mock of this belief, to me it brings
> Nor fear, nor grief, nor vain perplexity.
> So will I build my altar in the fields,
> And the blue sky my fretted dome shall be,
> And the sweet fragrance that the wild flower yields
> Shall be the incense I will yield to Thee,
> Thee only God! and Thou shalt not despise
> Even me, the priest of this poor sacrifice.

From these instances of the psychological curiosity

contesting with the spiritual creed in Coleridge's
nature-poems I must turn to the fragmentary revela-
tion of his published journals. The first remark
which these induce me to make is that we have
never had a more gifted watcher of the countenance
of Nature, or listener to her soliloquies, than Coleridge; the "nocturnal reveries" in *Anima Poetæ* are
to me the most intense and communicative things
of their kind in English. Their vital intimacy is
due in part to a faculty of their author convention-
ally denied him—realism. Watery moonlight is "as
if it had been painted and the colours had run";
grief a medley "of which the real affliction only plays
the first fiddle"; he looks at "the blue, yellow, green
and purple-green sea, with all its hollows and swells,
and cut-glass surfaces," his robin is "sweet cock-my-
head-and-eye, pert-bashful darling." In the earlier
part of *Anima Poetæ* he is often describing the
night-sky and rumour of the Lakes, and were he to
do no more we could hear him for ever on the subject:
"The voice of the Greta and the cock-crowing.
The voice seems to grow like a flower on or about
the water beyond the bridge, while the cock-crowing
is nowhere particular—it is at any place I imagine and
do not distinctly see. A most remarkable sky! the
moon, now waned to a perfect ostrich egg, hangs

over our house almost. . . . The break over the house is narrowed into a rude circle, and on the edge of its circumference one very bright star. See! already the white mass, thinning at its edge, *fights* with its brilliance. See! it has bedimmed it, and now it is gone, and the moon is gone. The cock-crowing too has ceased. The Greta sounds on for ever. But I hear only the ticking of my watch in the pen-place of my writing-desk and the far lower note of the noise of the fire, perpetual, yet seeming uncertain. It is the low voice of quiet change, of destruction doing its work little by little."

Without further indication we know in such passages that Coleridge, apart from dejection, accepts the phantasm of Nature in itself, as an expression not of mere physical experiment but of a "strange Power" akin to Emily Brontë's vision. His own endless complexity of eye and mind's eye restrains him from forming any settled shape of devotion. Presently he comes nearer to that single solution. "In looking at objects of Nature while I am thinking, as at yonder moon dim-glimmering through the dewy window-pane, I seem rather to be seeking, as it were *asking* for, a symbolical language for something within me that already and for ever exists,

than observing anything new. Even when that latter
is the case, yet still I have always an obscure feeling
as if that new phenomenon were the dim awaking
of a forgotten or hidden truth of my inner nature.
It is still interesting as a word—a symbol. It is
Logos the Creator, and the Evolver." Let us try to
catch him again making a point at the theologic
Nature. Midnight of March 2nd, 1805. "What a
sky! the not yet orbed moon, the spotted oval, blue
at one edge from the deep utter blue of the sky—a
MASS of *pearl*-white cloud below, distant, and travel-
ling to the horizon, but all the upper part of the
ascent and all the height such *profound* blue, deep
as a deep river, and deep in colour, and those two
depths so entirely *one*, as to give the meaning and
explanation of the two different significations of the
epithet. Here, so far from *divided*, they were
scarcely *distinct*, scattered over with thin, pearl-white
cloudlets—hands and fingers—the largest not larger
than a floating veil! Unconsciously I stretched forth
my arms as to embrace the sky, and in a trance I had
worshipped God in the moon—the spirit, not the
form. I felt in how innocent a feeling Sabeism might
have begun. Oh! not only the moon, but the depths
of the sky! The moon was the *idea*; but deep sky
is, of all visual impressions, the nearest akin to a

feeling. It is more a feeling than a sight, or, rather, it is the melting away and entire union of feeling and sight!" The consciousness of Coleridge will never rest, but in its passage through this existence it makes as many discoveries for us as any one genius will ever make; it is "infinite finiteness" and only fails to sway the world with one vast intellectual manifesto because itself is in unpausing evolution, in change of view and faculty like a sunrise.

The rapidity of Shelley, who knew his own affinity with Coleridge, is not so subject to metamorphosis. Great thinker as he was, he had a fixed plan—fixed, that is, within the laws of all mutability,—and because of it was empowered to complete works of art, and confessions of faith. Having seen a spirit, he was not compelled by the scientific side of his nature to proceed with its material equation; he could preserve its radiance long enough to be understood by others in symbol and in intimation.

Mont Blanc yet gleams on high: the power is there.

He almost refuses to admit the human advantage of too urgent and ambitious an attempt on the unknown.

Lift not the painted veil which those who live
Call Life.

Better, perhaps, for the majority to retain their idols than to live in the wilderness waiting to wrestle with dark angels. Better for himself, after nearly thirty or three hundred years of passionate negotiation with the dynasts, of star-gazing and unbinding Prometheus, to be "rocked round in earth's diurnal course." The "Ode to the West Wind," it is true, concludes with a prayer apparently for the dispatch of Shelley's opinion of political justice into all the corners of the earth; and that desire fulfilled could only come to good. But I do not think that this most cloud-compelling Ode had its inception in any of Shelley's enthusiasms for the human race. It was an abnegation and a return; we have all felt something of this wild release in the majesty of some autumn tempest. The moment comes when the works of reason and the concerns of civilisation seem the unreality, and that which is abroad in the moors and on the face of the waters is the magnetic reality. All the world seems in the secret—and are not we? "To what strange altar, O mysterious priest?" The eye of the mystery is on the mortal:

> If I were a dead leaf thou mightest bear;
> If I were a swift cloud to fly with thee;
> A wave to pant beneath thy power, and share

The impulse of thy strength, only less free
Than thou, O uncontrollable! If even
I were as in my boyhood, and could be

The comrade of thy wanderings over Heaven,
As then, when to outstrip thy skiey speed
Scarce seemed a vision; I would ne'er have striven

As thus with thee in prayer in my sore need.
Oh, lift me as a wave, a leaf, a cloud!
I fall upon the thorns of life! I bleed!

A heavy weight of hours has chained and bowed
One too like thee: tameless, and swift, and proud.

The destroyer is also the preserver; the fountain will restore Shelley, send him back with new vibration to his own life as the west wind of human action.

Had he done no more for us than sing of his skylark and cloud, his dancing stars and dædal earth, we should have been his debtors for a brightness in the sky and an elixir in the rain. His poetry is "one with Nature" in the sense that the skylark was "sprite or bird"; he is that to which Leigh Hunt compared the new-classical Keats, "a shape out of the old mythology," the human embodiment of a force in Nature. Whatever his wonderful and trained intellect might say in defence of freedom, in promotion of sympathy, in prophecy of achievement could scarcely exceed the elemental argument of his lyrical translucency. Man is known for a bad habit of driving angels from his door; he almost drove Shelley away, but could not. The catcalls "Atheist," "Polygamist," "Anarchist" could not howl down the music that flew so swiftly, so strongly, so tenderly into English constancy.—This incarnate fiend and indecent Radical—but stay, is this his? Charming, I admit. Charming. Bless my heart, *that's* Shelley's. (Old gentleman, and proud of his flower-garden, reads. His son from Cambridge watches with a seraphic grin, if seraphs grin:)

> And in the warm hedge grew lush eglantine,
> Green cow-bind and the moonlight-coloured may,
> And cherry-blossoms, and white cups, whose wine
> Was the bright dew, yet drained not by the day;
> And wild roses, and ivy serpentine,
> With its dark buds and leaves, wandering astray;
> And flowers azure, black, and streaked with gold,
> Fairer than any wakened eyes behold . . .

The old gentleman knows that this witness is true, and that it will not be long before Thomson's "Seasons" is not the gospel of Nature in English poetry. He goes on upbraiding Shelley for a heathen and a rebel; he is at it here and there to this day; but he makes sure that he has the Poems in the library, next to those of Coleridge.

While Shelley is ethereally eloquent of the "wandering by the way," and for glowing landscape or for flowery garland or the posy of a ring not excelled, he perhaps more than our other poets soars away into the spheres. It is not so much imagination as what Coleridge specifies as "coadunation" which takes him into the orbit of the worlds on worlds that are rolling ever.

> An azure mist
> Of elemental subtlety, like light,

gives him ubiquity; I do not know what futurity has in store for us of natural sensation and phenomenon not granted to the solid (or sullied) flesh of this present, but should not be amazed to find that Shelley had given a recognisable prelusion of those.

> To cheer our state
> He bids ascend those subtle and fair spirits
> Whose homes are the dim caves of human thought,
> And who inhabit, as birds wing the wind,
> Its world-surrounding æther: they behold
> Beyond that twilight realm, as in a glass,
> The future: may they speak comfort to us.
> *Look, sister, where a troop of spirits gather,*
> *Like flocks of clouds in spring's delightful weather,*
> *Thronging in the blue air!*
> > *And see! more come,*
> *Like fountain-vapours when the winds are dumb,*

That climb up the ravine in scattered lines.
And, hark ! is it the music of the pines ?
Is it the lake ?   Is it the waterfall ?
'Tis something sadder, sweeter far than all.

Having had Shelley, what has this race to fear? What act in the long drama dares it not see unrolled? What may we hesitate to leave behind of all the richness and "unspeakable security" of Nature here?

A ship is floating in the harbour now,
A wind is hovering on the mountain's brow;

there is a steersman who knows his course, and the rising of unalterable if uncharted stars.

THE PASTORAL DREAM

Spenser, Shakespeare, Milton, W. Browne,
T. Hood, Tennyson, M. Arnold

"There is scarcely any species' of poetry," wrote
Dr Johnson in 1750, "that has allured more readers,
or excited more writers, than the pastoral." He
proceeds to explain that. Pastoral is a way out of
"cares and perturbations" into "Elysian regions,
where we are to meet with nothing but joy, and
plenty, and contentment; where every gale whispers
pleasure, and every shade promises repose." And
why not? Must that word "stark" be always
ringing in our ears? There was once a modern
reviewer who decided to avoid the word. Unfor-
tunately he sent an article to the press with what
should have read "star-talk" in it. The printers
knew that some one had blundered. Stark talk it
was, and there it was.

The pastoral escape has suffered in our esteem

because too frequently those professing to make it have merely followed a prepared track leading into a large wardrobe, full of the relics of the imitators of Theocritus and Virgil. While it is not impossible for a poetic pleasure to thrive in English dialogues between Strephon and Chloe, or Hylas and Ægon in a musical competition for a goat and a vase, yet those names are prognostics of nonsense, and the whole arrangement is frigid and cramped. If we are to have anything of the sort, if shepherds and shepherdesses must be our means of hearing how the stars shine and brooks murmur, then let us have the correct local circumstance; let our shepherds be those recommended by John Gay, who gather no other nosegays but what are the growth of our own fields; sleep under no myrtle shades, but under a hedge; do not vigilantly defend their flocks from wolves, because there are none. The pastoral quality in our poetry, however, is another matter still from the "Shepherd's Week" in which Gay at once ridicules the *ferme ornée* poets and shows something of the affairs and recreations of Hodge and Lucy.

Pastoral is a fine and lucky essence, drawn from deeper wells than the milking-pail and dewier light

than the blueness of bonny Susan's eye; it is a
music beyond the tabor of Tom and Ciss, or,
if you prefer the argument in more modern dress,
the roundabout and jazz band of what to-day's
shepherd calls a "gala." It brings perfect freedom
with it:

> Soft as breezy breaths of wind
> Impulses rustle through the mind.

It is the secret of our fairy land, the metamorphosis
of the moonbeams playing through the stirred
foliage of the oak into Oberon and Titania and their
court. It is the instant arrival at our Hesperides,
our Avilion, our other country where the "small
unsightly root" and dark and prickled leaf bears the
golden flower.

The mazes of "The Faerie Queene," with which
Palgrave in his pleasing notebook on landscape in
our poetry expresses some disappointment, are
softly luminous with this pastoral, this dream that
waits for seers like Spenser. The country is
known, yet unknown. The shrill cock warns it,
not so much that day is coming, as that Phœbus
is coming. There is a lion behind the elm-tree,
and wood-gods behind the horned oak branch
out their horned heads. The vanity of this place

is perhaps

> To laugh at shaking of the leaves light,
> Or to behold the water worke and play
> About our little frigot, therein making way.

A little cottage of sticks and reeds holds a witch. And

> There where the mouldred earth had cav'd the banke,
> And fast beside a little brook did pass
> Of muddie water, that like puddle stanke
> By which few crooked sallows grew in ranke,

the sound of clanging hammers tells us to expect "some blacksmith"; it is Care forging Unquiet Thoughts. In the darkest shadow of the wood, a fair face gleams out like the sun. Three friends gathering strawberries are attacked by a tiger, which a shepherd lays low with his crook. I would not be bold enough to say that the "Faerie Queene" is universally of one sustaining fantasy, but to me much of it appears like a summer wandering through the world's-end tracks and farms and lodges of England, permitted to propose to the adventurer's geniality something a little more than the common realisation, a myth and a transcending.

In Shakespeare this "willing suspension of disbelief," this unprisoned pride of fancy, this spiritual discernment among English landscapes, is found in a more creative harmony, with still richer conception of common sight and vision. The dark, stubborn, uncouth, toilsome character of Nature is Caliban, and the gay, free, charming, unsubstantial grace is Ariel. There, the bark of the tree, and there, its music in the south-west wind. *The Tempest* is English pastoral at its ultimate pitch. For the woodland, there is one god who says,

> I pr'ythee, let me bring thee where the crabs grow;
> And I with my long nails will dig thee pig-nuts;
> Show thee a jay's nest, and instruct thee how
> To snare the nimble marmozet; I'll bring thee
> To clust'ring filberts, and sometimes I'll get thee
> Young scamels from the rock.

That is the wisdom of your earth-born. There is also the god who sings invisibly in the air, imitating the crowings of the barn-door fowl and the hounds and horn—sounds which we have heard, when on the bounds of the village, rather as dream voices than as familiar signs of rural affairs.

The *Midsummer Night's Dream* varies, and enriches, the interpretation of our forest lights and shades, our wild-flowers and changing moons, in a play of fairies. There is no Prospero now to give Puck his cue, but Puck is at liberty to run where he likes and bewilder lazy-witted folks. While he harasses the "hempen homespuns," like mischievous birds that perch on scarecrows to enjoy their thefts from the lands, the other fairies delight to guard sylvan innocence, to be commissioned spirits of

> dale, forest, or mead,
> Of pavéd fountain, or of rushy brook.

Call them star-beams, moonrays, ripples, dancing flowers, silver moths, sighs of air, the steps of field-mice on wheaten stems, dew-pearls on the leaf, perfumes of meadowsweet, gossamers, young birds waking—you will be right in a measure, for it is, I think, the experience of these and many other manifestations of solitude after the sun's remove that arises in Shakespeare's comprehension in form of elves,

> Following darkness like a dream.

We are never far from the hamlet and the gardens of the village; the bridle-way and stile-path are footed by the last labourers, while close by there lies the

> bank whereon the wild thyme blows,
> Where ox-lips and the nodding violet grows;
> Quite over-canopied with luscious woodbine,
> With sweet musk-roses, and with eglantine.
> There sleeps Titania . . .

In the *Winter's Tale* we are shown a lady more lovely in her thoughts than even Titania, but still a creation of the solitude of Shakespeare rather than his human experience. When Perdita is at her most entrancing, she is a spirit of the meinie of Flora; she is a flower become woman, or woman become flower, and her love blossoms into an air that no cloud can darken, nor summer's heat nor winter's tooth molest, all in flowers;

> Daffodils
> That come before the swallow dares, and take
> The winds of March with beauty; violets dim
> But sweeter than the lids of Juno's eyes
> Or Cytherea's breath; pale primroses
> That die unmarried ere they can behold
> Bright Phœbus in his strength . . .

Tenderest and most durable of sensibilities, this faculty of Shakespeare's has created for us perpetual spring, and assured us of that enchanted ground which lies for ever a stone's throw from the inns and yards of the villages in this country, so happy in the partnership of Nature's handiwork and man's, in the peaceful neighbourliness of secrecy and familiarity.

The spell still works, though not with the same fountain-like freedom, in "The Sad Shepherd" of Ben Jonson and "The Faithful Shepherdess" of Fletcher. "A certain Dorique delicacy," as Sir Henry Wotton called it, was among the feelings which the Elizabethan masters possessed in general. Wotton was particularly referring to "Comus," which, among its other honours, has that of being a vision of English countryside after the fall of night, and coming of

> the gray-hooded Even,
> Like a sad votarist in palmer's weed.

These things are hardly metaphors. They are the conclusions of the heart, when the eye has gazed long and the ear has forgotten the diurnal significances of the rumours which it hears. The contemplation, and the hallucination, unite in the poetry. Two worlds at once, nothing less, are what the imagination of a Milton commands. Of one, the "plain facts," no delineation could be clearer:

> Might we but hear
> The folded flocks penn'd in their wattled cotes,

Or sound of pastoral reed with oaten stops,
Or whistle from the lodge, or village cock
Count the night watches to his feathery dames,
'Twould be some solace yet, some little cheering,
In this close dungeon of innumerous boughs.

These we hear. We hear besides the "wonted roar" of strange and desperate thoughts, dreary powers of darkness. And then at last we hear, from nightingale, chaste lady, or angel, that sound which

            stole upon the air, that even Silence
Was took ere she was ware, and wish'd she might
Deny her nature, and be never more,
Still to be so displac'd. I was all ear,
And took in strains that might create a soul
Under the ribs of Death . . .

The mask of "Comus" was presented at Ludlow Castle in 1634. Two books of *Britannia's Pastorals*, by William Browne of Tavistock, had been published and republished by that time. These long poems are not distinguished by that new-fashioning genius of Milton, but they are wonderful in their simpler wooing of Nature and the spirit of our country retreats, which speaks in a personifying cordiality. The music of Nature, for example, is reported under the notion of a concert:

Two nights thus pass'd: the lily-handed Morn
Saw Phœbus stealing dew from Ceres' corn.
The mounting lark (day's herald) got on wing,
Bidding each bird choose out his bough and sing.
The lofty treble sung the little wren;
Robin the mean, that best of all loves men;
The nightingale the tenor, and the thrush
The counter-tenor sweetly in a bush.
And that the music might be full in parts,
Birds from the grove flew with right willing hearts;
But (as it seem'd) they thought (as do the swains,
Which tune their pipes on sack'd Hibernia's plains)
There should some droning part be, therefore will'd
Some bird to fly into a neighb'ring field,
In embassy unto the King of Bees,
To aid his partners on the flowers and trees,
Who, condescending, gladly flew along
To bear the bass to his well-tuned song.
The crow was willing they should be beholding
For his deep voice, but being hoarse with scolding,
He thus lends aid: upon an oak doth climb,
And nodding with his head, so keepeth time.

It is a lover's tale, an ingenuity, not a vision, but
founded in a delightful understanding and old
acquaintance.

Having spoken on an earlier occasion of William
Collins, I do not introduce him now; neither will
I attempt to discover precisely the pastoral delight

and revery of Shakespeare in other eighteenth century writers on Nature who ought to be in my chronicles. Gray has succeeded in leaving us the most frequently quoted verses on a landscape, an atmosphere, a time of day that we have; and yet I do not find him departing from the beaten way of observation. The noble numbers which open the "Elegy" are carefully chosen, and convey the less profound sense of Evening and labour's release and the vanities of human ambition with extreme taste and art. There is no admission of the spirits of Nature among the workings of Gray's mind; the landscape is one thing, the watcher another. Goldsmith's "Deserted Village" is, in the days of its felicity, very succinct and respectable. Its charms are chiefly indoors or on the green; no wood-god comes in reach of the constable, and no daffodil rises magically without the industry of "the swain responsive as the milkmaid sung." The bittern and lapwing are made into mere signs of hard times, and no hint given that they are capable of anything but dullness. This is not the English pastoral. Christopher Smart fathoms more deeply; there is a flowery jubilation and flash of wings and burst of piping in his later poems, especially the

"Song to David." His world would go on and be alive and warm even if his village was deserted; he honours the infinity of animation, as his garden or his hedgerow shows it, with direct and daring lyrical detail.

Yet let me take this occasion to pay a tribute to Thomas Hood, as a man attuned to those influences of Nature which the earlier and greater poets felt, and gifted to perpetuate his pastoral insight in melodious verse. Hood's serious poetry has not passed by without being recognized in the main; but in the general award it is his brief style that matters. I wish, I own, that more knowledge of his longer poems was apparent nowadays. The longer poems include several which, if one is lucky, harmonise with the emotions and divinations caused by certain places, and circumstances in Nature. "The Plea of the Midsummer Fairies," in its graceful intricacies and its entire creativeness of natural piety, is too little read, although Lamb, who followed out the course of the true pastoral in this country, found it so near the old excellence as to make him write a "Tale from Thomas Hood" in prose upon it. Allowing the sadder and stranger instincts of his genius to discover their counterpart, Hood also wrote the unrivalled

"Haunted House" and "The Elm Tree, a Dream in the Woods"—unrivalled, I mean, in their peculiar discrimination of the occult in English landscape and amenity.

> But busy bees forsake the Elm
>   That bears no bloom aloft—
> The finch was in the hawthorn-bush,
>   The blackbird in the croft;
> And among the firs the brooding dove
>   That else might murmur soft.
>
> Yet still I heard that solemn sound,
>   And sad it was to boot,
> From every overhanging bough
>   And each minuter shoot;
> From rugged trunk and mossy rind,
>   And from the twisted root:
>
> From these, a melancholy moan;
>   From those, a dreary sigh;
> As if the boughs were wintry bare,
>   And wild winds sweeping by,—
> Whereas the smallest fleecy cloud
>   Was steadfast in the sky.

The comparative obscurity of such men as Hood and George Darley, who like him had the fairy sympathy, was due to the arrival of Tennyson as the poet of his times—the delightful writer who knew what not to say, what not to demand. Presumably no man could have been other than that which he was, but Tennyson without his caution and his poeticising should have created work of much more radiant vitality than all his proud collection. Having chosen his track, however, he could not recede. He harnessed up Romance and Policy, and the result became similar to Mark Twain's "Court Gazette from Camelot":

> Monday the King rode in the Park,
> Tuesday the King rode in the Park,
> Wednesday the King rode in the Park,

and so on. By turning the Muse into a cloak, he did not improve his final fortunes as a poet. How wonderfully would Tennyson have written, if he had written reluctantly and under the real descent of the Promethean flame! As it is, he has crowded artificiality upon his original beauties. His pastoral itself, promising to combine all the reports of fine sense, and perception, and shadowy apprehension, drifted into a compilation of natural history jottings, to be thrust into his versification at a pinch. From Parnassus he patiently worked his way down to the Gradus ad Parnassum.

This poet in his prime was visitable by visions of
Nature which will remain in their perfection.   He
had seen England as a mighty country not because
of her military superiority to the Dervishes but
because of her older presences.   He had stood before
the churchyard yew, and translated, or rather
allowed it to translate, its fibrous knotty life into
his consciousness, and utterance.   He had gone
alone to stare over autumn near and far:

> Calm and deep peace on this high wold,
>   And on these dews that drench the furze,
>   And all the silvery gossamers
> That twinkle into green and gold:

> Calm and still light on yon great plain
>   That sweeps with all its autumn bowers,
>   And crowded farms and lessening towers
> To mingle with the bounding main.

From those acceptances he withdrew into his didactic
office, seldom in later years treating Nature as the
poet who makes poets, but pleased, as Palgrave says,
if he felt that he had succeeded in putting into verse
some little-noticed phenomenon.   He "more than
once asked if I knew to what he referred," says
Palgrave, in the stanza,

Old warder of these buried bones,
  And answering now my random stroke
  With fruitful cloud and living smoke,
Dark yew, that graspest at the stones.

If that sort of curiosity were the test of poetry, there have been several hundred verse-writing naturalists who could claim to be Tennysons.

With the name of Matthew Arnold we return to the higher and deeper-nourished pastoral of England. I have not forgotten the metamorphosis of this poet into the inspector of schools. I have not forgotten the preface to his *Poems*, *1853*, with its sternly positive statement: "What are the eternal objects of poetry, among all nations, and at all times? They are actions; human actions . . ." But Matthew Arnold is being remembered chiefly as a poet of no actions, a Druid like Thomson; his permanent praise remains more or less defined in the phrase of A. H. Clough, who liked "The Scholar Gipsy" because it was "*so* true to the Oxford country." It is not necessary for me to elaborate that adverb of Clough's. Arnold is a poet of Nature, who makes use of the pleasant ghost out of Glanvill to engage the interests of his audience, and provide him with a semblance of action and the unity of his design;

but his real concern, theme, emotional and imaginative treasury is a landscape, and whatever is beckoning and singing within it, something not born for death. The Scholar is his Ariel, nor can we fancy or wish it otherwise; the Scholar is the secret friend of Nature and the poet, the hierophant of the dream, the breeze that brings the faint chimes to a clear tune and the forgotten flower-scent to a newness of experience. Pastoral with us, disdaining the mechanism of other times and regions, requires the concurrence of pure and modest country wisdom with the discovery, the fortunate discovery, of such allegorical figures as shall not darken a gleam or weaken a murmur of the labyrinthine simplicity at our town end.

THE FARMER'S BOY

S. Duck and R. Bloomfield

The conversation of the men who work on the land, when their topic is their life and experience, is full of translated colour and significant sound; it is with little difficulty that I have sometimes fancied, as I listened to three or four hearty haymakers, that there grew the true poem of Nature. Their whole sense seemed peculiarly trained to answer all that Nature in this country has to say or do, from the grasshopper's rustle to the assembly of the thunderstorm; their verbs seemed of the earth earthy, of the flowers flowery, and their illustrations of meaning simply added other depths of weather-beaten stoicism. We may define poetry as we will, but in the plain, shrewd, and curious eclogues which a subject like thrashing-tackle will set going in the country inn, there is an actuality of impression and a secret glory of soul which may scarcely be called anything but poetry.

It is now almost two hundred years since the first famous attempt on the part of the farm-labourer to conduct his poetical powers into higher surroundings and the strange field of publication. The name of Stephen Duck, the Thresher-Poet, has had time almost to die away even in the minds of book-hunters. It is worth while renewing it for a moment, and considering by the course of Duck's life and verse how the Farmer's Boy has made his painful and erroneous way into the dictionaries of biography. Duck was without any modification a labourer in Wiltshire during the early part of the eighteenth century, "engag'd" (says Spence) "in the several lowest Employments of a Country Life." His schooling had given him, however, reading and writing and some arithmetic. About 1724 Stephen began to be troubled at the rusty state of the arithmetic, and set about improving his mind. Working overtime, he obtained enough money beyond ordinary needs to buy three volumes of arithmetic, which he mastered. But this was only a stage in the transformation of Stephen. A friend from London assisted with a library of some two or three dozen books, including Josephus, Seneca, Ovid, and Bysshe's *Art of Poetry*. There was a Milton too, which the poet spelt out with frequent recourse to his dictionary. "Indeed," says Spence, "it seems plain to me, that he has got *English* just as we get *Latin*." Stephen toiled on, alike with flail and quill, and began to produce "scattered verses"; these by some magic (common in villages) could not be kept secret, and at length brought gentlemen from Oxford and clergymen from round about into the author's company. It is unnecessary within my present limits to trace the strange story of Stephen further in any nicety of detail; he became a beneficiary of the Queen, was ordained, published his poems with great applause and a strong list of subscribers, and twenty years later drowned himself in the Thames.

The *Poems on Several Occasions* of this remarkable person, issued in 1736, show all too plainly with what vain endeavour the Farmer's Boy who has unusual curiosity for mental experience elaborates his native style out of existence. If Duck could have been persuaded not to go out of his dialect, nor to seek a subject beyond the limits of his rural years and just imaginings, then we should

have had from him a report of Nature as she is in
the eyes of the closest witness. Her portrait, her
excellences, her whims, and her mysteries should
have been the matter of a georgic of sterner stuff
than Virgil's; the chance was brilliant. But neither
the poor smock-frocked poet, nor those partly
commendable ladies and gentlemen his patrons,
realised that "the voice of Nature" was possible
poetry. It is nothing surprising; men are continu-
ally missing the road in poetical judgment. The
early pages of Duck show the rapid extinction of the
poet of the fields, and the appearance of a trim
Horatian coupleteer. However, Stephen could not
metamorphose himself in an instant. His first-
printed piece "To A Gentleman," though practising
fluently on the usual plan—Parnassus' Summit,
Grecian Monarchs, the Trojan Race, a Favourite of
the Nine—is cut short by village reality:

> The Field calls me to Labour; I must go:
> The Kine low after Meat; the hungry Steed
> Neighing, complains he wants his usual Feed.
> Then, Sir, adieu.

Soon afterwards, Stephen receives from the Reverend
Mr Stanley a sensible suggestion that he should

write of his own work, and he does so, achieving what is his best piece for vigour and exactitude. Already, of course, some substitution has taken from his inbred expressiveness a deal of life; we must hear of Ceres' Gifts, and the Cyclops' Hammers. Yet on the whole "The Thresher's Labour" is a fair proposal for the poetry of the Farmer's Boy. The scene is antique and bold. The farmer commands with surly encouragement. The threshers know their enemies by old acquaintance—farmer, wheat, flail,—but they cannot choose. The earth is the ancient tyrant behind all this, and must be obeyed.

> No intermission in our Work we know;
> The noisy Threshal must for ever go.
> Their Master absent, others safely play;
> The sleeping Threshal does itself betray.

They think of the shepherd's hut and its "merry tale," of linnets singing, and streams playing; but these diversions are not for them. The farmer is hard as iron.

> He counts the Bushels, counts how much a Day;
> Then swears we've idled half our Time away:
> "Why, lookye, Rogues, d'ye think that this will do?
> Your Neighbours thresh as much again as you."

Now in our Hands we wish our noisy Tools,
To drown the hated Names of Rogues and Fools.
But wanting these, we just like School-boys look,
When angry Masters view the blotted Book:
They cry, "their Ink was faulty, and their Pen";
We, "the Corn threshes bad, 'twas cut too green."

Such is their winter work in the barn; in summer at last

Before the Door our welcome Master stands;
Tells us, the ripen'd Grass requires our hands.

This is good news, and the poet expresses well the sweet season before haymaking. But even here the sweet and bitter quickly blend; for the mowers find the heat of the day too great. After midday,

We often whet, and often view the Sun;
And often wish, his tedious Race was run.
At length he veils his purple Face from Sight,
And bids the weary Labourer Good-night.
Homewards we move, but spent so much with Toil,
We slowly walk, and rest at ev'ry Stile.
Our good expecting Wives, who think we stay,
Got to the Door, soon eye us in the Way.
Then from the Pot the Dumplin's catch'd in haste,
And homely by its Side the Bacon plac'd.
Supper and Sleep by Morn new Strength supply;

> And out we set again, our Work to try;
> But not so early quite, nor quite so fast,
> As, to our Cost, we did the Morning past.

The hayfield is notably animated; the agricultural year is a peaceful war, and after the squadron of mowers come the troops of haymakers, making, as the country-goer happily recalls, a pretty victory of it. Stephen Duck, honest soul, is of the commission; he shows the bustle and the play, and with that he is a rural wit—the "female throng" are grinned at by the mowers,

> Ah! were their Hands so active as their Tongues,
> How nimbly then would move the Rakes and Prongs!

Nature springs her little joke on these gossips while they sit at dinner; the breeze begins to moan, and down comes

> the thick impetuous Rain;
> Their noisy Prattle all at once is done,
> And to the Hedge they soon for Shelter run.
> Thus have I seen, on a bright Summer's Day,
> On some green Brake, a Flock of Sparrows play;
> From Twig to Twig, from Bush to Bush they fly;
> And with continu'd Chirping fill the Sky:
> But, on a sudden, if a Storm appears,
> Their chirping Noise no longer dins your Ears:
> They fly for Shelter to the thickest Bush;
> There silent sit, and all at once is Hush.

Fine sky shines through again, the triumph is crowned, the "glad Master" marshals his "safe Ricks." But still, the spearsmen of the bucolic army are not allowed long to cool themselves; the rhythm of the year is strong, and they must be moving again as reapers.   The cry is heard:

> "For Harvest now yourselves prepare;
> The ripen'd Harvest now demands your Care.
> Get all things ready, and be quickly drest;
> Early next Morn I shall disturb your Rest."

And the master is as good as his word; the reapers are summoned

to rise,

> While yet the Stars are glimmering in the Skies.

The Dawn shows them the wide beauty of the uncut corn; they

> Then look again, with a more tender Eye,
> To think how soon it must in Ruin lie!

They are not permitted long to consider the desolation that their coming means; they must in to it, under the beauty of morning, with twinkling villas and cottages peeping at them.

> The morning past, we sweat beneath the Sun;
> And but uneasily our Work goes on.

> Before us we perplexing Thistles find
> And Corn blown adverse with the ruffling Wind.
> Behind our Master waits; and if he spies
> One charitable Ear, he grudging cries,
> "Ye scatter half your Wages o'er the Land."
> Then scrapes the Stubble with his greedy Hand.

The taciturn bondmen hear with their ears. They know their place in the scheme of this hard mistress the land. They regard their master and his various tempers as like the weather or the soil. They pass on to their next labour.

> But soon we rise the bearded Crop again,
> Soon *Phœbus'* Rays well dry the golden Grain.
> Pleas'd with the Scene, our Master glows with Joy,
> Bids us for Carrying all our Force employ;
> When straight Confusion o'er the Field appears,
> And stunning Clamours fill the Workmen's Ears;
> The Bells and clashing Whips alternate sound,
> And rattling Waggons thunder o'er the Ground.
> The Wheat, when carry'd, Pease, and other Grain,
> We soon secure, and leave a Fruitless Plain;
> In noisy Triumph the last Load moves on,
> And loud Huzza's proclaim the Harvest done.

Now, it seems, the husbandman is in sight of a calm and plentiful holiday. The master gives the usual feast, and jugs of humming ale are pushed round so fast that the hireling forgets all his burdens.

But the next Morning soon reveals the Cheat,
When the same Toils we must again repeat;
To the same Barns must back again return
To labour there for Room for next Year's Corn.

On the whole, in that poem of the farm-hand's
year, Duck preserves the truth and maturity which
are the inimitable character of country conversa-
tions; forgetting that he is ambitious of rising
above his low station in life, he allows himself to be
the pipe for village experience to play upon; indeed
it is rather the earth, the plough, the sickle, the
grain, the flail, the body of the labourer that speaks
than the writer of the verses. How much richer
would the poetical harvest of two hundred years ago
have been, if these elemental forces had succeeded
in making Stephen their instrument more fully!
Unhappily, a barrier had been growing up between
the earth and her son and servant, and as we proceed
through Duck's *Poems* we look with but little
reward for more of that inspired simplicity. The
chirping thrush and finch, the swallows in airy
circles, the lurching mongrel worrying sheep, the
"ruffling Breezes cold" out of blushing skies, the
doves startled by "some Musquet's Thunder" into
separate and frightened tracks—these must all

depart while the exalted Thresher pays the most full-flourished compliments to "a Screen, worked in Flowers by her Royal Highness *Anne*, Princess of Orange," or "the Author of a Poem on the Duke of Lorain's Arrival at the British Court," or while he construes and imitates Horace. Once he essays a sounder subject—"A Journey to Marlborough, Bath, Portsmouth, &c."—though he must needs inscribe it to the Right Honourable the Lord Viscount Palmerston. But Stephen is altered. The grim Farmer is now

> "Kind *Menalcas*, Partner of my Soul."

There is a sad but pleasing incident on this gentle-man's land, which must be repeated in the ex-Thresher's own words:

> Breakfast soon o'er, we trace the verdant Field,
> Where sharpen'd Scythes the lab'ring Mowers wield:
> Straight Emulation glows in ev'ry Vein;
> I long to try the curvous Blade again.

He does, like King Lear:

> I snatch the Scythe, and with the Swains contest;
> Behind 'em close, I rush the sweeping Steel;
> The vanquish'd Mowers soon confess my Skill.

After that he attends the Threshers' Feast which Lord Temple has instituted in his honour, and he reflects

> Thus shall Tradition keep my name alive;
> The *Bard* may die, the *Thresher* still survive.

And the prophecy was right. In vain did Duck paraphrase Ovid and eulogize the great and good; in vain did he enjoy the thirty guineas a year which Queen Caroline gave him, or play his amiable part as country parson. His life had gone wrong, and his poetry with it; and so the Farmer's Boy of the Augustans passed by, hurrying from the consciousness of his unfortunate promotion and misdirected art.

I now turn to the more celebrated though not more remarkable Farmer's Boy of the early nineteenth century, in whom we may read something of the same ultimate error after similar indications of a genuine earth-born poetry. Robert Bloomfield is not a name to conjure with to-day. Once, however, he was as popular as Hardy; of his first poem, 26,000 copies are said to have been sold within three years. But he fails, in a severe examination, as his predecessor had done, through being lured out of his own world and speech into another where he met a host of superiors. Robert Bloomfield was son of the village tailor at Honington in Suffolk, and from about 1776 to 1781, when he was fifteen years old, was employed as a handy lad at Mr Austin's farm in the next parish. Whoever goes to those places will readily find the system of life and the spirit of the countryside little altered from what they were in Bloomfield's time. The stream, the mill, the ponderous horses and rambling geese and pigs, above all the soft brightness of the scene, may be recognised. Not promising to be hard enough for the full life of a farm-labourer, Bloomfield was sent up to London and his brother made a shoemaker of him. Both brothers developed a taste for reading, and writing; Robert borrowed Thomson's "Seasons." "I never heard him give so much praise to any book as to that," observes George. A dispute about apprenticeships compelled the youth to go back to Suffolk for a time, which was passed at Mr Austin's farm; then he returned to London and settled down or rather up in a garret with other shoemakers, working on ladies' shoes and composing in his mind a long poem called "The Farmer's Boy." When it had been written it was sent to that gallant gentleman and

pleasant bookman Capel Lofft, who had a farm at
Troston, near Bloomfield's home, and he finally
obtained its publication in 1800. Instantly the
work became the rage. By 1815 the 13th edition
was required; there were translations in French
("Le Valet du Fermier"), Latin, Italian; Bloomfield
had to meet the whims and advice of patrons. In
spite of this whirl of luck, he did not prosper greatly;
his subsequent books of verse were not very well
received, and we find him making not ladies' shoes
but Æolian harps for a living. He died in 1823, in
a state of melancholy and weakened mind.

Lamb thought that at the best of times Bloomfield
had "a poor mind," but this was hardly the point.
What Bloomfield might have been was the spirit of
the farm in our poetry, the prime of that delightful
rustic commentary on work and weather, legend and
character, which can so hardly be preserved in books.
It may be that without Thomson's "Seasons" to
show him the method of poetry, and the range of
observation and discussion already explored, Bloomfield would never have written "The Farmer's
Boy"; but it is also probable that the thinness and
platitude and external polish which are the poem's
defects, and which are so far removed from the

expressed enthusiasms of a farm-labourer in his own surroundings, are due to an exaggerated respect for the literary model. At any rate, with all its demerits, Bloomfield's picture of the farm and its figures year in and year out must be regarded as a phenomenal piece of work, and the little sheepish stumbling boy who went about Mr Austin's fields with so fresh a sensibility and emerged into a public of tens of thousands deserves our affectionate reconsideration. I shall pay him a tribute unusual in this hurried age by taking up his poem and making a note and an extract here and there.

It begins in Thomsonian tone, Goldsmithian measure:

> O come, blest Spirit! whatsoe'er thou art,
> Thou kindling warmth that hover'st round my heart,
> Sweet inmate, hail!

That is in feeling genuine, in utterance borrowed; but presently we come to the better and more homely style, introducing Giles. Mr Austin's kindness is at once acknowledged; the campaign before us will not be so harsh at all corners as that of poor Duck.

> No stripes, no tyranny his steps pursu'd;
> His life was constant, cheerful servitude:

Strange to the world, he wore a bashful look,
The fields his study, Nature was his book.

The farm is small but doing well; and the time is
Spring. Giles has many jobs, but among them he
has to look after the scarecrows, and this brings him
from bed first thing; then he joins like a young bird
in the chorus along the sandy sunk lane—all is
delicacy, variety, regeneration:

Stopt in her song perchance the starting Thrush
Shook a white shower from the black-thorn bush,
Where dew-drops thick as early blossoms hung,
And trembled as the minstrel sweetly sung.

With the budding and the gleaming all round, Giles
sets his scarecrows dangling, and gets back to the
house; there through the noise of pigs and ducks
and turkeys he hears the dairymaid's bawl "Go
fetch the Cows." Off he goes to the meadow and
halloos them into the yard, in their usual precedency;
then under the morning sun he has to help in the
milking beside singing Mary:

And crouching Giles beneath a neighbouring tree
Tugs o'er his pail, and chants with equal glee;
Whose hat with tattered brim, of nap so bare,
From the cow's side purloins a coat of hair,
An unambitious, peaceable cockade.

This ended, he is

> A *Gibeonite*, that serves them all by turns:
> He drains the pump, from him the faggot burns;
> From him the noisy Hogs demand their food,
> While at his heels run many a chirping brood,
> Or down his path in expectation stand
> With equal claims upon his strewing hand.

How gentle and how powerful is this kind of harmony with Nature! As one reads, one almost demands nothing more complete and enigmatic. Meanwhile, the boy becomes a shepherd, as the year grows serene and leafage darkens; he has to see to it that the pasture fences are whole, but even in that there is a rapture:

> High fences, proud to charm the gazing eye,
> Where many a nestling first essays to fly;
> Where blows the woodbine, faintly streak'd with red,
> And rests on every bough its tender head;
> Round the young ash its twining branches meet,
> Or crown the hawthorn with its odour sweet.

The boy turns from this fairy-piece to his young lambs at play, and all his young impulses are with them:

> A bird, a leaf will set them off again,
> Or, if a gale with strength unusual blow,
> Scattering the wild-briar roses into snow,

> Their little limbs increasing efforts try;
> Like the torn flower the fair assemblage fly.

While he sees the blown petals, and the petal-like lambs, he is struck by another parallel and a painful one; for here comes "the murdering Butcher with his cart." Poor Giles is to see his "gay companions" huddled off to the knife and block.

Summer now enters, and, from the poetical point of view, not at all well:

> The Farmer's life displays in every part
> A moral lesson to the sensual heart . . .

But we need not emphasise those errors of education which dull and cramp the youthful image of Giles, with whom we go off to turnip-sowing after a night of light rain; that task of faith accomplished, it is the boy's duty to hunt the sparrows out of the corn which they invade with a gay impudence, under "the leafy thorn." And here, after giving them a fright, he loiters, for he loves the place, and Wisdom loves him for loving it. Now for something like pecking with the sparrow, and more permissible:

> Just where the parting bough's light shadows play,
> Scarce in the shade, nor in the scorching day,
> Stretcht on the turf he lies, a peopled bed,
> Where swarming insects creep around his head.

The small dust-colour'd beetle climbs with pain
O'er the smooth plantain-leaf, a spacious plain!
Thence higher still, by countless steps convey'd,
He gains the summit of a shivering blade,
And flirts his filmy wings, and looks around,
Exulting in his distance from the ground.
The tender speckled moth here dancing seen,
The vaulting grasshopper of glossy green . . .

Giles longs to have a sharper sense of these little lives, but is called up by the skylark, starting from the corn, and soon in and out of the light cloud, and higher in the blue,

His form, his motion, undistinguish'd quite,
Save when he wheels direct from shade to light:
E'en then the songster a mere speck became
Gliding like fancy's bubbles in a dream—

for the child-farmer falls asleep. The year goes on with bounty; the reapers, gleaners come, and Giles now has to work like a slave at carting the corn. He still has feelings for the troubles of others, and laments the cruelty which has docked "poor patient Ball" of his tail, and left him there in the blaze while the flies freely suck his blood. A small thing in this great world, not so small in that farmyard; where then the poor cow, already tormented by the gadfly,

is assailed by the spiteful gander and tyrannised.
Humour, however, is there too. "The strolling
swine" engages this braggart bird;

> Whose nibbling warfare on the grunter's side
> Is welcome pleasure to his bristly hide;
> Gently he stoops, or stretcht at ease along,
> Enjoys the insults of the gabbling throng . . .

From this serio-comedy of the strawyard the boy
raises his face to the setting sun and fantasied "fiery
treasures" of clouds in the west; gets to bed, but at
midnight wakes to the onset of thunder, and the
rising wind in the full-leafed elms, and the whim-
pering mastiff. Then the cool, and music of the
easy rain, and harvest's last morning, and harvest-
home.

But woods turn yellow, and the year declines.
Giles lets out the cleanly pigs among the oaks, and
sometimes knows where they are, and watches their
pleasures and alarms; the wild duck's eye like a gem
meets his as she sits alone, and then she springs up
in fear, and they in fear

> decamp with more than swinish speed,
> And snorting dash through sedge and rush and reed:
> Through tangling thickets headlong on they go,
> Then stop and listen for their fancied foe;

Giles loses them when they herd under the roosting-bough of the pheasant, and cannot with "his piercing call" bring them in.   It is a time of wild shades and excitements; of labour too, such is the mysterious wheel ever revolving with this world of farms, and swine, and boys—the plough and tumbril are out on the clogging mould, and leisure only comes when

> the distant chime
> Of Sabbath bells is heard at sermon-time
> That down the brook sound sweetly in the gale,
> Or strike the rising hill, or skim the dale.

Even the church is part of the farms; straw-roofed, broken-windowed, its stones tufted with mallows and nettles, its tower usurped by grey-capped daws, it is all an outhouse and a hovel of the earth-life. Now, as the days grow dangerous, Giles would wish to be at the fireside, warming the farmyard weaklings as himself is warmed; but fate is against him.   He is sent with a shotless gun to drive off the rooks from the sprouting wheat, dawn to dusk; and all alone in the lee of the thinned hedge he shivers, until he has a boyish inspiration.   A little hut of turf and thatch, a fire of sticks, and sloe and hip to roast at the fire; he sets about the work, and finishes it.   And now he obtains the promise of his junior urchins at the green

to come and play "the Crusoe of the lonely fields"
with him.   He makes up the seats for "the coming
guests"; the branches of berries sputter over the
flame; "he sweeps his hearth."   The guests fail
him, and he stares over the solitude in vain.

The fourth season and last canto of "The Farmer's
Boy" opens according to foolish plan with some
unlucid moralisation, from which we are pleased to
be rescued even by the lowing of cattle in frozen
pastures, and the thud of swedes tumbled out of the
cart by poor Giles in the sleet.   Not that the moral
itself was a bad one; but the humanitarian gospel
according to our Suffolk labourer is best presented in
picture and anecdote.   The winter farm described
in that way is indeed a home of equality, and all
ranks—two-legged, four-legged, winged or woolly—
appear in kindly mutual comprehension.   The ewe
and heifer must wait on Giles to break the ice and
let them begin on their turnips, and when night falls
there is often an innocent trick played on him by the
hungriest:

> From him, with bed and nightly food supplied,
> Throughout the yard, hous'd round on every side,
> Deep-plunging Cows their rustling feast enjoy,
> And snatch sweet mouthfuls from the passing Boy,

Who moves unseen beneath his trailing load,
Fills the tall racks, and leaves a scatter'd road;
Where oft the swine from ambush warm and dry
Bolt out, and scamper headlong to the sty,
When *Giles* with well-known voice, already there,
Deigns them a portion of his evening care.

This done he creeps in among the farmer's family
and servants by the hearth, for which he has helped
bring the faggots and logs; and even here, if he
lacks anything in natural community of feeling with
his animals, he must listen to his master "mild as
the vernal shower" on the subject, and his spirit
must range the farm to be assured that he has failed
in nothing. The horsekeeper, who has heard all
this before, drops to sleep in his corner, but presently
starts, and calls Giles to take a walk with him:

Ever thoughtful of his team,
Along the glittering snow a feeble gleam
Shoots from his lantern, as he yawning goes
To add fresh comfort to their night's repose;
Diffusing fragrance as their food he moves,
And pats the jolly sides of those he loves.

Besides this Giles must make sure of his sheep, in
fear of some mastiff or cur that has found a taste for
murder; and this duty, unpleasantly dragging him

from the fireside, may sometimes have a touch of
wonder in it, "if the full-orbed Moon salute his
eyes." A universalising fancy occurs to him, which
not the deepest mystic would be ashamed to share,
as he looks at the silvered stillness above, and the
ranges of clouds

> Spotless as snow, and countless as they're fair;
> Scatter'd immensely wide from east to west,
> The beauteous semblance of a *Flock* at rest.
> These to the raptur'd mind, aloud proclaim
> Their MIGHTY SHEPHERD's everlasting Name.

But, with the rural mind, idea does not preside
long at a stretch, and Giles is brought "from plains
of light to earth" in another fancy. "A grisley
SPECTRE, cloth'd in silver-gray" stands along the
lane among waving shadows, and the owl flies with
terrifying invisibility and cry above him. He
stands to arms, and is not unrewarded; the ghost
vanishes, and all that is there is an old friendly ash—

> Slowly, as his noiseless feet draw near,
> Its perfect lineaments at once appear;
> Its crown of shivering ivy whispering peace
> And its white bark that fronts the moon's pale face.

Thus on he goes again with kind angels through the
winter nights, and winter cannot last for ever; the

primrose will not be daunted, the lambs come, and at the dawn beside their ewes

> Those milk-white strangers bow the trembling knee.

To find them out sheltered sunshine and promising valleys will now carry his heart on into the spring; to be praised for his cares and vigils

> By gazing neighbours, when along the road,
> Or village green, his curly-coated throng
> Suspends the chorus of the Spinner's song

will reward him wholly and complete his course. Yet never must that completion be an ending— all is in advance,

> "*Another* Spring!" his heart exulting cries,
> "*Another* Year!"

Deep and happy riddle, solved by him with painful work, and trials and fears, and something like the vision which sends the new sap into the hedge and gold into the sky.

Such is the principal poem of Bloomfield, and while it often suffers from the imposition of a literary language and philosophical convention alien to his old usages, and never completely mastered by his "poor mind," while it might have been more incisive and indeed imaginatively adequate if it had been voiced in a series of lyrical ballads, yet altogether it is the Farmer's Boy speaking. Of him this country should be proud. He will be in heaven before the majority of us, even authors and lecturers, and will be in his element with the verification of Isaiah's pastoral; he is our Melampus, and when (through Bloomfield) I have heard the story of his heart, I do not know that any union with Nature could be more desirable than his. If civilisation kills him, so much the worse for civilisation. Of Bloomfield's subsequent poems of Nature, I shall not at present speak; many of them illuminate this actual idyll, but none can rival its tenacious contentment in the bosom of the earth and the silken or woolly or feathered sides of her children committed to the charge of human children.

VI

THE SELBORNIAN

GILBERT WHITE AND SOME PREDECESSORS AND SUCCESSORS

IT is not necessary to make a noise in order to win immortality. Retirement can achieve that. On the appearance of White's *Selborne* in 1789 the Warden of Merton College observed to the nephew of the naturalist, "Your uncle has sent into the world a publication with nothing to call attention to it but an advertisement in the newspapers; but depend upon it the time will come when very few who buy books will be without it." At first the prophecy seemed doubtful of fulfilment. It was thirteen years before the first octavo edition extended the public acquaintance with Selborne. It was forty years before the book began to be included in series of popular reprints. But with the Victorian era its day had fully come; it became like Walton's *Angler* and the *Pilgrim's Progress* a work which editors loved to supplement and discuss, artists to adorn with vignettes and plates, and publishers to produce in as fresh and fitting a style as they could devise. Little more than a century after the original issue of this book, the manuscript appeared in the saleroom, where it changed hands for £294 or about the same sum as at that time was given for the holograph of Keats's "Lamia." We have a Selborne Society as the final tribute of this nation of society-formers to a country clergyman who valued his parish.

The discovery that one need not range the world in order to teach the world—or, if teaching is an obsolete expression, to give pleasure and promote openness of sympathy—was considerably older than Gilbert White, although to us he is so intimately associated with it. Being but an indifferent student of the ancient world, I cannot identify the first Selbornian

In Tempe, or the dales of Arcady;

I must content myself with allusion to the much later friend of Nature and seclusion, Virgil. The *Georgics* have had a longer and wider reign even than the *Natural History of Selborne*. They are superficially addressed to Maecenas, but their best spirit is that of the easy philosopher

> By himself walking,
> To himself talking.

Their world is a parish, and Virgil its parson, without a tithe-barn. Down on the farm the business and bigness of Rome has drifted away, and a sudden importance has invested the bee-hive and the shoots of corn. If one moves about quietly and without egotism, one will be permitted to see things which are cleverer than mechanical pumps and more instructive than the scrolls of the school-men. There are some deep questions here too, which have an answer in eternity probably affecting the whole course of human development. Person-ality flows in these channels, springs on these wings, speaks in these contests and encounters.

During the eighteenth century, and much later, Virgil's rural and physico-theological poetry was read with attention, and affection, by the young men of England. The schoolmaster of Gilbert White was the Rev. Thomas Warton, a pleasant poet and classic, and father of two men who largely recommended the Virgilian aspect of the country to the general imagination, Joseph and Thomas Warton. The effect of Thomas Warton, Senior, on his pupils was apparently considerable. In 1753 Joseph Warton, of Oriel College, Oxford, produced his agreeable edition of Virgil in English verse with numerous dissertations and comments, praising Virgil (in the Dedication) for "giving life and feeling, love and hatred, hope and fear, wonder and ambition, to plants and to trees, and to the very earth itself: and for exalting his favourite insects, by endowing them with reason, passions, arts and civil government." In 1789 Gilbert White of the same College revealed himself as the prose Virgil of England, and did not so much presume to *give* animation to the inhabitants of his tithe-map as to receive it from them by virtue of a supreme modesty, a constant curiosity, and a sense of worlds within worlds.

If he had had Virgil for his predecessor, he had had the access of other poets more recent to whom he owed some passages in the shaping of his temperament and mode of expression. It is the serenely unerring beauty of White's natural history which has caused many whose natural history is small to read him every year. His results are stated with the poetic justness and delicacy of word, passage, pause, and cadence. We may be sure that he strengthened his inherent command of scientific method by devoted familiarity with John Ray—incidentally, the forerunner of our veneration and love for the South Downs; and with William Derham, whose *Physico-Theology* came to a thirteenth edition in 1768. White mentions them both, for example, in the Letter of June 18th, 1768. But neither Ray nor Derham could assist him much in the perfection of his crystal-clear or his mezzotint styles, his gentle confidence of description, and his restrained but long-lingering utterances of emotion.

> If aught of oaten stop, or pastoral song,
> May hope, chaste Eve, to soothe thy modest ear,

it is White's. Let me repeat a little of that sober music now, at the risk of interrupting the argument —a paragraph from the letter written on behalf of his tortoise Timothy:

"Know then, tender-hearted lady, that my great misfortune, and what I have never divulged to anyone before, is the want of society with my own kind. This reflection is always uppermost in my mind, but comes upon me with irresistible force every spring. It was in the month of May last that I resolved to elope from my place of confinement; for my fancy had represented to me that probably many agreeable tortoises, of both sexes, might inhabit the heights of Baker's Hill, or the extensive plains of the neighbouring meadow, both of which I could discern from the terrace. One sunny morning I watched my opportunity, found the wicket open, eluded the vigilance of the gardener, and escaped into the sainfoin, which begun to be in bloom, and thence into the beans. I was missing eight days, wandering in this wilderness of sweets, and exploring the meadow at times. But my pains were all to no purpose; I could find no society such as I sought for. I began to grow hungry, and to wish myself at home. I therefore came forth in sight, and surrendered myself up to Thomas, who had been inconsolable in my absence." We have had some modern compositions on the same subject of tortoises in love, but I am much mistaken if White's is not at once more true to Nature and more resourceful and accomplished in the art of re-creating things by words.

But now I revert to the poets whose characteristic excellences agreed with White's enthusiasm for Nature and made his style sweeter. He came into a literary world which was beginning to be enchanted with the minor poems of Milton.   The chastities of "Comus" were at their priest-like task, and those sylvan presences lured fancy on without demands for elaborate powers of genius.   Half a dozen poets had been emboldened by the master to be sensitive of landscape and the glances and voices of Nature, and to follow him in a verse that played along quite innocently and happily in its own bounds.   Matthew Green, John Dyer, David Mallet, William Blackstone (the titanic Hand of the Law), the Wartons—these were some of the Miltonidaè.   Dyer particularly in "Grongar Hill" had expressed the mood of a solitary and contented observer:

> Grass and flowers Quiet treads,
> On the meads and mountain-heads,
> Along with Pleasure, close ally'd,
> Ever by each other's side:
> And often, by the murm'ring rill,
> Hears the thrush, while all is still,
> Within the groves of Grongar Hill.

It was the emerging of the new nature-worship that his flowing picture-verse revealed, the assurance that one small corner of England unknown to fame was sufficient for studies, delight, and works of art. Later on, becoming a country clergyman, Dyer with more laborious mind and in less transparent verse proclaimed the shepherd's life. "The Fleece," though unwieldy and turbid, contains such moments of self-lost rustic contemplation, and opinion on Nature's rights, as to be worthy of Selbornian parallels. The calendar which frames Dyer's sheep and shepherds is exceedingly fresh and evocative:

> If verdant elder spreads
> Her silver flow'rs; if humble daisies yield
> To yellow crow-foot, and luxuriant grass,
> Gay shearing-time approaches . . .

> And the weakest, in thine arms,
> Gently convey to the warm cote, and oft,
> Between the lark's note and the nightingale's,
> His hungry bleating still with tepid milk.

It is to Thomson, however, that White recurs in his *Selborne*. "The Seasons," which lately receives little except ironical attention, may be as a whole a generalisation, a wide and rhetorically impressive composition, in which Nature is often approached by proxy, and books and prints intervene between the poet and the bright restless truth. That passage on the nightingale, for example, mourning her stolen nest, would be more touching if we did not feel the ambition of poetic artfulness, after classical models, too clamant in it. But we cannot deny to Thomson a great number of new and vivid testimonies of direct response to the life around him. He was, in White's opinion, and that is opinion enough, "a nice observer of natural circumstances." To be that is to be a human being with a difference. Thomson in his free hours is what Collins called him—a Druid, a spirit of the woods. His sense is delicate then:

> Gradual sinks the breeze
> Into a perfect calm; that not a breath
> Is heard to quiver through the closing woods,
> Or rustling turn the many-twinkling leaves
> Of aspin tall.

Then he can with great insight share the destinies and feelings of wild life, can scheme and fear and tremble with the hunted hare,

> Shook from the corn, and now to some lone seat
> Retired; the rushy fen; the ragged furze,
> Stretched o'er the stony heath; the stubble chapp'd;
> The thistly lawn; the thick-entangled broom;
> Of the same friendly hue, the withered fern.

But whether in his drowsier passages or in his vital moments, Thomson had something more to implant in the age of Gilbert White. It was Shakespeare's hint, "sermons in stones," but carried on into a way of living. There was no sectarian intention in Thomson; "The Seasons" was not even a specifically Christian poem. But it was a confession of faith, a doctrine of the fullness of life; and by its richness, its learning, and its marshalled meditation it trained the eighteenth century towards Nature, emotionally, poetically, scientifically. The infinite book of secrecy was made easier to open, and the young mind was persuaded that the wonderful was not remote, the beautiful not limited. After Thomson, it was not difficult to feel with rapture that

> The flowery leaf
> Wants not its soft inhabitants. Secure
> Within its winding citadel, the stone
> Holds multitudes.

The biped superiority of man was brought into better terms with the other sons of God. Thomson in his closing Hymn, with a noble Benedicite of his own, maintained, what so many great naturalists and travellers would soon show in action, that there was no "farthest verge of the green earth" to which he would not cheerfully go—

> I cannot go
> Where Universal Love smiles not around,
> Sustaining all yon orbs and all their sons;
> From seeming evil still educing good,
> And better thence again, and better still,
> In infinite progression.

It was in this spirit that Gilbert White arose and went, though not to the farthest verge, not even to Innisfree, but to Selborne, " in the extreme eastern corner of the county of Hampshire, bordering on the county of Sussex, and not far from the county of Surrey."

Eighteenth-century clergymen were ready writers. While Sterne was addressing Eliza and publishing the *Sentimental Journey*, while James Woodforde was filling up his *Diary*, Gilbert White was producing in his handsome unhurried script the folio pages of letters to Thomas Pennant which with others to Daines Barrington were to be his great book. Though given to the public in 1789, *The Natural History of Selborne* began in 1767. The opening note is that of dignity and contentment; Selborne is described topographically with the serious care that might have been bestowed on North America. Here, says White, is my microcosm. You did not

perhaps think that a "poor pelting village" had so
many aspects, but you must learn, as White has
done. You did not think that this part of England
possessed sublimity, but you are wrong: it boasts
"the vast range of mountains, called the Sussex
Downs," and "Nore Hill, a noble chalk promontory,
remarkable for sending forth two streams into two
different seas," one into the British Channel, and
one by way of the Thames into the German Ocean.
The nature of the soils, the wells, the timber is
quickly sketched, and suggests the primitive an-
tiquity of Selbornian needs; here man is at once the
servant and master of Nature, and looks on her face
for the signs of his good or bad luck. Necessity
and philosophy unite at once at Selborne.

That is the ground on which the first letter sets
our feet, and in the second we are shown what
Nature can do at Selborne. She grew the Oak in
the Plestor, "a vast oak, with a short squat body,
and huge horizontal arms," under which the
peasantry passed their leisure, the old folks in chat
and the young in dance and antic. That Oak,
however, was brought to the ground by the "amaz-
ing tempest in 1703." The Power that made, could
destroy. And then White speaks of another oak,

the Raven Tree, which is to introduce us to the society of Selborne—and its tragedies.   Man decided to fell this stronghold of the raven.   "It was in the month of February, when those birds usually sit. The saw was applied to the butt, the wedges were inserted into the opening, the woods echoed to the heavy blows of the beetle, or mallet, the tree nodded to its fall; but still the dam sat on.   At last, when it gave way, the bird was flung from her nest; and though her parental affection deserved a better fate, was whipped down by the twigs, which brought her dead to the ground."

The third letter hints how the geologist can discover the primal history in Selborne ploughlands; the fourth, how local craftsmen turn Nature to account;   the fifth is a panegyric of Selborne's appeal to the intelligence, local patriotism at its finest, beginning with the "wild appearances" and "various botany" of the sunk roads, and ending in the tune of the Psalmist, "The inhabitants enjoy a good share of health and longevity; and the parish swarms with children."   Then our parson takes a slight, and genial, liberty.   The Forest of Wolmer is not wholly in his parish, but it is one of its most remarkable blessings.   He leads us into it, in four letters; records its legends, defines its attractions, loiters by its "considerable lakes," and stands in rapture among the willows to survey its "vast flocks of ducks, teals, and widgeons, of various denominations, where they preen, and solace, and rest themselves, till towards sunset." And now that we know our Selborne as an area fairly well, he enters into other matters. He is a scientist, harassed, he says, by the want of neighbours skilled in "natural knowledge." He makes a series of observations on the birds, fishes, quadrupeds, reptiles, and plants of Selborne, and invites comprehending discussion; endeavours to test grand theories by his parochial observation, and again modestly inquires if his gleanings may lead to main discoveries of natural principles.

At the end of the twenty-fourth letter, White returns to his old love, Poetry, and addresses to Pennant his couplets entitled "The Naturalist's Summer Evening Walk." Here he with simplicity echoes the Countess of Winchilsea,

> When curlews cry beneath the village-walls
> And to her straggling brood the partridge calls,

and Thomson, and Joseph Warton, and Collins, and

the Milton of "L'Allegro" and "Il Penseroso," and
Pope in Windsor Forest, and the ancients; and yet
he contrives to remain Gilbert White of Selborne.
The piece is significant to a commentator on White
because it indicates the part played by poets in
educating his attitude and way of writing, especially
the melody and correctness of his prose.

Letter XXV is superscribed "To the Hon.
Daines Barrington," who from this time shares
White's correspondence with Pennant, and begins
with a definition of White's function—he "pro-
fesses to be an outdoor naturalist, one that takes his
observations from the subject itself, and not from
the writings of others." Then comes a list of
summer and winter "birds of passage"—migrants—
which in a hasty view looks like any other catalogue,
but in fact is not, for White's sweetness and good
humour cannot be excluded even from his briefest
phrases. Thus,

Less reed-sparrow. A sweet polyglot, but hurrying; it
has the notes of many birds.
Woodcock . . Appears about old Michaelmas.

As the correspondence proceeds, there is no lack of
incident or experiment, but I shall not pause here

until Letter LVI, which is heretically dated not from Selborne but from Ringmer, near Lewes, December 9th, 1773. White is on his travels, and rejoicing in the Sussex Downs, "that chain of majestic mountains." As he dilates on their beauties, he gives us an idea and a speculative style as spacious as something in Sir Thomas Browne: "Perhaps I may be singular in my opinion, and not so happy as to convey to you the same idea, but I never contemplate these mountains without thinking I perceive somewhat analogous to growth in their gentle swellings and smooth fungus-like protuberances, their fluted sides, and regular hollows and slopes, that carry at once the air of vegetative dilatation and expansion; or, was there ever a time when these immense masses of calcareous matter were thrown into fermentation by some adventitious moisture,—were raised and leavened into such shapes by some plastic power, and so made to swell and heave their broad backs into the sky, so much above the less animated clay of the wild below?"

The spirit of wonder never deserted this comfortable clergyman; rather, as he grew older, it grew more powerful in him. In 1775 he recounts his memory of a surprising shower of gossamer on

September 21st, 1741, not, he is quick to explain, out of superstitious troublings, but in the chronicle of Nature's innumerable possibilities. A little while afterwards, he writes the memoir of an idiot boy of his parish, whose hobby was bees: "They were his food, his amusement, his sole object." Thence he soon passes to dew-ponds, the mystery of the Downs. In 1778 he has a game with Echo, trying her ability with different sounds and from different points. "This village is another Anathoth, a place of responses, or echoes." Echo, who finds no great difficulty with Latin verses, is soon presented with another problem, when a friend of White's fires off his three swivel guns towards the Hanger. The effect is small; so the guns are placed on the Hanger and fired, and this time "the sound, rushing along the Lythe and Comb-wood, was very grand; but it was at the Hermitage that the echoes and repercussions delighted the hearers, not only filling the Lythe with the roar, as if all the beeches were tearing up by the roots, but turning to the left, they pervaded the vale above Comb-wood ponds; and, after a pause, seemed to take up the crash again, and to extend round Harteley Hangers, and to die away at last among the coppices and coverts of Ward-le-ham."

When the crack of doom summons us, White will be there, congratulating the Almighty in his most courteous nature-phrase on the phenomena vouchsafed to the intelligent observer.

The closing letters, six of them, form a gallery of weather displays at Selborne. We began with the friendly character of the village, we close with the inscrutable but still observable countenances of greater Nature, to whom Selborne and Siberia are equally submissive. Great frosts and snowfalls overtake us now; Gilbert's cat becomes electrical, and his Sunday joint freezes; or by contrast we are thrust into fierce droughts and thunderous calms and storms. White is careful not to theologise these for his readers. He paints the scenes, and leaves us to form our deductions. He has been awakening our affections and our admirations through the series of letters, and this is his last invocation. We went to Selborne in quiet every-day weather, we are leaving it in smouldering light, red stubborn fog, or pouncing lightnings and rushing hailstones. All, in short, that the Creator chooses to disclose to man's senses, passions, and dreams in this life is within the realm of a parson in a country parish; and having shaped his long design so well, White "takes a respectful leave of you and Natural History together" on June 25th, 1787.

These sentiments concerning White have, of course, borne no colour of being complete in any way; I have not spoken of the shrewdness of his conjectures and his anticipations of subsequent certainties—as when he precedes Darwin in the recognition of earth-worms among the world's best workers. His one famous error, that on the where-abouts of the swallow-kind in winter, accompanied him to his grave; but it seems to have been due to his affection for poetry rather than temporary indifference to the evidence. A passage in Thomson (who enjoyed the poetic use of the improbable) was surely concerned in it. Leaving aside these issues, I come to the effect that White's life-work had on England. When the power of Thomson's "Seasons" was waning, that of *Selborne* was growing, and, since prose of White's companionable kind is easier than verse to be read in length, it was finding its way to a wider class of thinking persons. White was very largely responsible for the fact that at one time hardly any periodical publication was without its column on Natural History; and the much more glorious fact that with all his paradoxical misdeeds the Englishman carries with him wherever he goes an honour of Nature, whether in the form of a bird, a tree, an animal, or a landscape. He may improve his distinction still, but White's modest miracle is still in operation.

With the doctrine (too severe a term!) of White, that of William Cowper was entirely harmonious, and there is a consonance between the literary grace of these two hermits, these country gods. *The Task* was published four years before *Selborne*, and has vied with it in the number of its editions. In the first Book, Cowper beautifully opens the mind to his landscapes, sounds, and sweet airs, and declares the happy effect of Nature on human nature, and the curse that attends life spent without that inspiration. His only complaint of rural life appears in the fourth Book: "The town has tinged the country." The two concluding Books are his walks in winter, which lead him not merely to re-create, with a serenity all the more wonderful if we recollect the anxieties of his religious state, the masques and intimations of Nature in England, but also to make a poetic speech on the subject of man's conduct towards Nature. These tranquil old gentlemen of Selborne or Olney can speak with an intense eloquence when they are moved to do so. The "familiar nightcap" falls from Cowper's head when he confronts mankind with this "thing to say" on animal's rights, and I fancy a thorny crown takes its place. He is against the gentleman with the gun on all counts; accepting his Bible and the state of evolution, he agrees heartily with human pre-eminence, but "the groans of Nature in this nether world" are at our door;

> We are held
> Accountable; and God some future day
> Will reckon with us roundly for the abuse
> Of what He deems no mean or trivial trust.

It is what Mr Ralph Hodgson said, in his own forceful manner, in a modern poem, founded partly on the scientific justification since Cowper's day of that warning. But Cowper claims no prophetic fame.

> I am recompensed, and deem the toils
> Of poetry not lost, if verse of mine
> May stand between an animal and woe,
> And teach one tyrant pity for his drudge.

From the combining leadership of Selborne and Olney, several poets quickly took example, and before the year 1800 their quiet works on, in, and for Nature were abundant and were appreciated. Two of these were in a manner neighbours of Gilbert White. James Hurdis, curate of Bishopstone in Sussex, printed his "Favourite Village" in 1800, not long before his early death. There is a prospect of an edition of Hurdis, whose exceedingly rich observation and understanding of Nature deserve such a memorial. The unlucky Charlotte Smith was also of Sussex, and wrote a poem in blank verse on "Beachy Head," exquisitely garlanded with her beloved flowers:

> With rays like golden studs on ivory laid
> Most delicate: but touch'd with purple clouds,
> Fit crown for April's fair but changeful brow.

Another example of the poetry consequent on White and Cowper is that now discarded but once favoured book of Thomas Gisborne, *Walks in a Forest*. Ten editions were called for. Its poetic elixir may be in doubt, but not the variety of its lively notes from Nature, and the enchantment that belongs to a man who is perfect in his own paths. Gisborne went into his woods with an absolute receptiveness of what was passing there.

It is necessary to mention Crabbe, though no

pretence of an estimate of that great poet must be suspected, in this conjunction. "The Village" had appeared before *Selborne* and before *The Task*. It was an ironical counterblast to Goldsmith's "Deserted Village," and concerned the human interests of a poor parish almost exclusively. Then, or soon afterwards, Crabbe was not found among the publishers' lists. His later work is much more obviously imbued with the pursuits and predilections of White and of Cowper. Crabbe was an exact naturalist, and a happy one; and he learned that his parish not only included the foul backyard and the seducer but also the charities, the charms, and endeavours of Nature apart. Then he could give us "the least speck upon the hardest flint" as a triumph and a mystery, or make his seashore brilliant with its weeds that sparkle and waves that blaze; or he could lurk with the birds of the fen among the salt reeds.

From White's rectory the light shone far in other directions, and I have detained my audience too long to plan out the matter. The authors of books in prose, suggested or supported by his book's fascination, are too many and too good for a summary. But I must name some names, which I hope

I shall never think of without pleasure and gratitude: J. L. Knapp, author of the *Journal of a Naturalist*; Jeffreys Taylor with his little books on *The Farm* and collateral subjects; Mary Roberts and her *Annals of my Village*; Mary Mitford with *Our Village* and her thousands of constituents; Edward Jesse, kindliest of rangers, though his introduction to White's *Selborne* is slatternly; Charles Waterton, wittiest of them all, not excepting Frank Buckland; Leonard Jenyns of Swaffham Bulbeck; Edward Newman, printer, and "Rusticus" of Godalming; Thomas Miller the basket-maker, and maker of "sunny spots of greenery" too; the ubiquitous William and Mary Howitt; Canon Atkinson tramping the moors; A. E. Knox on his *Ornithological Rambles*; C. A. Johns in the woods or at the Lizard, J. G. Wood—sometimes; Edward Buxton in Epping Forest, or J. R. Wise in the New Forest; Richard Jefferies in sight of a watermill or a gamekeeper's larder; Mr Collett, or Mr Massingham. These names I throw out at random are only a few of the multitude, which does not stop at the coast of England, but voyages up the Amazon and with the *Beagle*; I barely indicate the type of writers and books in the succession of Gilbert White, and a library of the best English kind, both for substance and embodiment, which is still within the reach of those who must watch other precious volumes carried afar with imperious inevitableness. We need the virtues of Gilbert White and his Selbornian men and women very keenly at this moment of a threatened national character; and there is no obstacle to prevent us from close contact with them. There never was any obstacle between White and the complete Englishman.